KRISHNA MOHAN AVANCHA

Developing a Phoenix Brand!

First edition

This book was professionally typeset on Reedsy.
Find out more at reedsy.com

Contents

1

Introduction: What is a Phoenix Brand?

Introduction: What is a Phoenix Brand?

In today's rapidly changing business landscape, companies are constantly striving to create brands that can withstand the test of time. One concept that has gained popularity in recent years is that of the Phoenix brand, which is a brand that rises from the ashes of its own failure to become even stronger than before. In this article, we will explore what a Phoenix brand is, why it matters in today's business landscape, and the key themes and topics that will be covered in the book.

Defining a Phoenix Brand

A Phoenix brand is a brand that has experienced significant failure or setback but has been able to reinvent itself and come back stronger than ever before. This type of brand is named after the mythical bird, the phoenix, which is said to be able to rise from its own ashes and regenerate itself. Examples of Phoenix brands include Apple, which faced a major setback in the 1990s but was able to reinvent itself with the launch of the iPod and iPhone, and Netflix, which transformed itself from a DVD rental service into a streaming giant.

Why Phoenix Brands Matter

In today's business landscape, where disruption and innovation are constant, the ability to reinvent oneself is crucial. The lifespan of a company is getting shorter, and the average tenure of a company on the S&P 500 index is now less than 20 years. With the rapid pace of technological change and shifting consumer preferences, companies need to be able to adapt quickly or risk being left behind. Phoenix brands demonstrate that failure is not the end, but rather an opportunity to learn, grow, and come back even stronger.

Key Themes and Topics

The book will cover a range of key themes and topics related to Phoenix brands, including:

1. Understanding Failure: One of the key themes of the book will be the importance of embracing failure and using it as a learning opportunity. We will explore case studies of companies that have experienced failure and how they were able to turn it into a positive experience.
2. Reinvention: The ability to reinvent oneself is a crucial aspect of building a successful Phoenix brand. We will explore the different strategies that companies can use to reinvent themselves, from product innovation to re-branding.
3. Customer centricity: Phoenix brands are often able to succeed because they are able to truly understand

their customers and their needs. We will explore the importance of customer centricity in building a successful Phoenix brand.

4. Leadership: Leadership is another key aspect of building a successful Phoenix brand. We will explore the characteristics of effective leaders and how they can help guide their organizations through times of change and uncertainty.

5. Innovation: Innovation is a crucial aspect of building a successful Phoenix brand. We will explore the different strategies that companies can use to foster a culture of innovation, from design thinking to agile development.

Phoenix brands are a crucial aspect of modern business, given the rapid pace of technological change and shifting consumer preferences. They offer a powerful example of how failure can be transformed into success by embracing it as an opportunity to learn, grow, and reinvent oneself. In this article, we will explore the key themes and topics related to Phoenix brands that will be covered in the book.

Understanding Failure

The first theme of the book is the importance of understanding failure. Many companies view failure as something to be avoided at all costs, but in reality, failure is an inevitable part of any innovation process. Companies that are willing to embrace failure and use it as a learning opportunity are better equipped to succeed in the long run. The book will explore case studies of companies that have experienced failure and how they were able to turn it into a positive experience. By understanding failure, companies can build resilience and become more adaptable in the face of change.

Reinvention

The ability to reinvent oneself is a crucial aspect of building a successful Phoenix brand. Companies that are able to adapt quickly to changing market conditions are more likely to survive and thrive in the long run. The book will explore the different strategies that companies can use to reinvent themselves, from product innovation to rebranding. By embracing new ideas and being open to change, companies can create a culture of innovation that enables them to stay ahead of the curve.

Customer Centricity

Phoenix brands are often able to succeed because they are able to truly understand their customers and their needs. By putting the customer first, companies can create products and services that truly resonate with their target audience. The book will explore the importance of customer centricity in building a successful Phoenix brand. By listening to customer feedback and using data to inform decision-making, companies can create products and services that meet the needs of their customers and stand the test of time.

Leadership

Leadership is another key aspect of building a successful Phoenix brand. Effective leaders are able to guide their organizations through times of change and uncertainty, inspiring their teams to embrace new ideas and take calculated risks. The book will explore the characteristics of effective leaders and how they can help build a culture of innovation within their organizations. By creating a vision for the future and inspiring their teams to work towards that vision, leaders can help their organizations achieve long-term success.

Innovation

Innovation is a crucial aspect of building a successful Phoenix brand. Companies that are able to continuously innovate are better equipped to stay ahead of the curve and adapt to changing market conditions. The book will explore the different strategies that companies can use to foster a culture of innovation, from design thinking to agile development. By encouraging experimentation and being open to new ideas, companies can create a culture that enables them to continuously innovate and stay ahead of the competition.

Conclusion

Phoenix Brands offer a powerful example of how failure can be transformed into success. By embracing failure, reinventing oneself, and putting customers first, companies can build brands that are resilient, adaptable, and capable of withstanding the test of time. The book will explore these themes and topics in-depth, providing readers with insights and strategies for building their own Phoenix brands.

2

The Power of Branding: Why It Matters

The Power of Branding: Why It Matters

Branding is an essential aspect of any business, big or small, and can significantly impact its success. The process of branding involves creating a unique name, design, symbol, or image that identifies and differentiates a product or service from others in the market. A strong brand can create a positive reputation, enhance customer loyalty, and increase the perceived value of a product or service. This article discusses the importance of branding and provides examples of successful brands that have leveraged branding to their advantage.

Creating a Unique Identity

Branding creates a unique identity for a business and its products or services. A well-crafted brand can convey a message about a company's values, mission, and vision, which helps customers to connect with the brand on a deeper level.

Customers are more likely to remember and relate to a brand that has a distinct identity and stands out from its competitors. This is particularly important in crowded markets, where businesses need to differentiate themselves to succeed.

For example, Apple is a company that has created a strong brand identity that is instantly recognizable. Its sleek and modern design, minimalist logo, and focus on innovation have made it a leader in the tech industry. By creating a unique identity, Apple has been able to stand out in a crowded market and maintain a loyal customer base.

Building Trust and Loyalty

Branding can help to build trust and loyalty with customers. A strong brand conveys reliability, quality, and consistency, which are essential in building long-term relationships with customers. Customers are more likely to choose a brand they trust and have had positive experiences with in the past. This leads to repeat business and recommendations to others, which can significantly impact a business's success.

Coca-Cola is a brand that has built trust and loyalty with its customers over many years. Its logo, colors, and packaging are instantly recognizable, and the brand is associated with good times and happy memories. Coca-Cola's marketing campaigns have reinforced this image, making it one of the most successful and recognizable brands in the world.

Increasing Perceived Value

Branding can also increase the perceived value of a product or service. A strong brand can create a perception of quality, exclusivity, and desirability, which can justify a higher price point. Customers are often willing to pay more for a product or service that they perceive to be of higher quality or value.

Luxury brands like Rolex and Louis Vuitton have leveraged branding to their advantage by creating a perception of exclusivity and luxury. Their products are associated with high quality and are often priced accordingly. Despite the higher price point, these brands have been able to maintain a loyal customer base and continue to grow.

Conclusion

Branding is a powerful tool that can significantly impact a business's success. A strong brand can create a unique identity, build trust and loyalty with customers, and increase the perceived value of a product or service. By leveraging branding to their advantage, businesses can differentiate themselves from competitors, maintain a loyal customer base, and increase their revenue. Some of the most successful brands in the world, such as Apple, Coca-Cola, Rolex, and Louis Vuitton, have used branding to their advantage and become household names. Therefore, it is important for businesses to invest in branding to build a strong reputation and achieve long-term success.

Quick examples:
Apple

Apple is a prime example of a company that has used branding to its advantage. Its brand identity is built around simplicity, innovation, and sleek design. Apple's logo, a bitten apple with rainbow colors, is simple yet memorable and has become one of the most recognizable logos in the world.

Apple's branding strategy has been consistent across all its products, from the Mac computer to the iPhone and iPad. This consistency has helped to create a strong brand identity that customers associate with quality, innovation, and exclusivity. Apple's branding has enabled it to stand out in a crowded market and maintain a loyal customer base that eagerly anticipates its latest product releases.

Coca-Cola

Coca-Cola is a brand that has become synonymous with happiness and good times. Its branding strategy is built around creating a positive emotional connection with customers. Coca-Cola's logo, colors, and packaging are instantly recognizable and evoke feelings of nostalgia and happiness.

Coca-Cola's marketing campaigns reinforce its brand identity by emphasizing the social aspect of drinking Coca-Cola. Its "Share a Coke" campaign, for example, encouraged customers to share a Coke with their friends and family, reinforcing the brand's connection with happy moments and memories.

Rolex

Rolex is a luxury brand that has built a strong brand identity around exclusivity, quality, and precision. Its logo, a crown, is simple yet powerful and has become a symbol of luxury and success. Rolex's branding strategy is built around creating a perception of exclusivity, which justifies its high price point.

Rolex's marketing campaigns reinforce its brand identity by emphasizing its association with successful people and events. For example, Rolex is the official timekeeper of Wimbledon and the Australian Open, reinforcing its connection with high-end events and successful individuals. Rolex's branding has enabled it to maintain a loyal customer base that is willing to pay a premium for its high-quality watches.

Louis Vuitton

Louis Vuitton is a luxury brand that has built a strong brand identity around quality, exclusivity, and elegance. Its logo, LV, is instantly recognizable and has become a symbol of luxury and high fashion. Louis Vuitton's branding strategy is built around creating a perception of exclusivity, which justifies its high price point.

Louis Vuitton's marketing campaigns reinforce its brand identity by emphasizing its association with high fashion and style. Its campaigns often feature famous models and celebrities, reinforcing the brand's exclusivity and high-end status. Louis Vuitton's branding has enabled it to maintain a loyal customer base that is willing to pay a premium for its high-quality and exclusive products.

3

Defining Your Brand Identity: Who Are You and What Do You Stand For?

Defining Your Brand Identity: Who Are You and What Do You Stand For?

A brand identity is the collection of attributes and values that define a company or organization's personality, culture, and mission. It is what sets a brand apart from its competitors and creates a connection with its customers. Defining a brand identity is a crucial step in building a successful business, as it helps establish a consistent message and image across all marketing channels. In this article, we will discuss the process of defining a brand identity, including identifying values, mission, and vision. We will also offer guidance on how to conduct a brand audit to determine your current brand identity.

Identifying Values, Mission, and Vision

To define a brand identity, you must first identify your company's values, mission, and vision. These three components are essential in creating a brand identity that resonates with your customers and aligns with your business goals.

Values are the guiding principles that shape your company's culture and behavior. They are the beliefs and ideals that your organization holds dear and seeks to uphold. To identify your company's values, ask yourself what drives your business and what you want to be known for. Examples of common values include integrity, innovation, creativity, and teamwork.

Mission is the reason your company exists. It is the statement that defines your purpose and communicates your unique selling proposition. A well-crafted mission statement should answer the question, "What does your company do?" and "How does it benefit your customers?" A clear and concise mission statement can help guide your company's decision-making and keep everyone focused on achieving the same goal.

Vision is the long-term goal or future state that your company aspires to achieve. It is the "big picture" that you want to create, and it should be inspiring and motivational. A compelling vision statement can help align your team's efforts and create a sense of purpose and direction. To create a vision statement, ask yourself what you want your company to achieve in the next five or ten years.

Conducting a Brand Audit

Once you have identified your company's values, mission, and vision, the next step is to conduct a brand audit. A brand audit is an evaluation of your current brand identity to determine its strengths, weaknesses, and opportunities for improvement. It involves analyzing your brand's messaging, visual identity, customer perception, and competitive positioning.

Here are some steps to conduct a brand audit:

1. Review your brand messaging: Your brand messaging includes your mission statement, tagline, and key messages. Review these elements and ensure that they are consistent with your values, mission, and vision. Also, evaluate how effectively they communicate your unique selling proposition and differentiate your brand from competitors.
2. Assess your visual identity: Your visual identity includes your logo, color palette, typography, and graphic elements. Evaluate whether your visual identity is consistent across all marketing channels and whether it effectively communicates your brand's personality and values.
3. Analyze customer perception: Conduct market research to understand how your customers perceive your brand. Use surveys, focus groups, or online reviews to gather feedback on your brand's strengths, weaknesses, and areas for improvement.
4. Evaluate competitive positioning: Research your competitors to understand how they position themselves in the market. Analyze their messaging, visual identity, and pricing strategy. Identify opportunities to differentiate your brand and stand out from the competition.
5. Develop a brand strategy: Use the insights gained from the brand audit to develop a brand strategy that aligns with your values, mission, and vision. Identify key messaging and visual elements that will differentiate your brand and resonate with your target audience.

A brand identity is the collection of attributes and values

that define a company or organization's personality, culture, and mission. Let's take Apple Inc. as an example. Apple's brand identity is defined by its innovative and user-friendly products, sleek and minimalist design, and a focus on customer experience.

Identifying Values, Mission, and Vision

To define a brand identity, you must first identify your company's values, mission, and vision. These three components are essential in creating a brand identity that resonates with your customers and aligns with your business goals.

Values are the guiding principles that shape your company's culture and behavior. They are the beliefs and ideals that your organization holds dear and seeks to uphold. Let's take the outdoor clothing and gear company Patagonia as an example. Patagonia's values include environmental responsibility, sustainability, and activism. These values are reflected in their products and marketing campaigns.

Mission is the reason your company exists. It is the statement that defines your purpose and communicates your unique selling proposition. Let's take Airbnb as an example. Airbnb's mission is to create a world where anyone can belong anywhere. This mission statement communicates their goal of creating a more connected and inclusive world through travel.

Vision is the long-term goal or future state that your company aspires to achieve. It is the "big picture" that you want to create, and it should be inspiring and motivational. Let's take Tesla as an example. Tesla's vision is to accelerate the world's transition to sustainable energy. This vision statement communicates their goal of creating a more sustainable future through innovation.

Conducting a Brand Audit

Once you have identified your company's values, mission, and vision, the next step is to conduct a brand audit. A brand audit is an evaluation of your current brand identity to determine its strengths, weaknesses, and opportunities for improvement.

Here are some steps to conduct a brand audit:

1. Review your brand messaging: Let's take Coca-Cola as an example. Coca-Cola's messaging is focused on creating happiness and moments of togetherness through their products. Their "Taste the Feeling" campaign emphasizes the emotional connection that people have with the brand.

2. Assess your visual identity: Let's take Nike as an example. Nike's visual identity includes their iconic "swoosh" logo, the "Just Do It" tagline, and a focus on bold and inspiring visuals. This visual identity is consistent across all marketing channels and effectively communicates Nike's values of athleticism and empowerment.

3. Analyze customer perception: Let's take Amazon as an example. Amazon's brand is associated with convenience, reliability, and a vast selection of products. A customer perception analysis might involve analyzing customer reviews and feedback to identify areas where Amazon can improve their customer experience.

4. Evaluate competitive positioning: Let's take McDonald's as an example. McDonald's competitive positioning is focused on offering affordable and convenient fast food. Their brand messaging emphasizes their iconic products,

such as the Big Mac and the Happy Meal, and their widespread availability.

5. Develop a brand strategy: Let's take Starbucks as an example. Starbucks' brand strategy is focused on creating a "third place" between home and work where people can gather, relax, and enjoy a premium coffee experience. Their brand messaging emphasizes their commitment to quality, sustainability, and community involvement.

Conclusion

Defining a brand identity is a critical step in building a successful business. By identifying your company's values, mission, and vision, and conducting a brand audit to evaluate your current brand identity, you can create a consistent and compelling brand identity that resonates with your customers and aligns with your business goals.

4

Crafting Your Brand Story: How to Tell a Compelling Narrative

Explanation in the form of a story:
Once upon a time, there was a small bakery in a quaint little town. The bakery had been around for decades, and it had always been known for its delicious baked goods. However, as time passed, the bakery found itself struggling to attract customers. People were no longer interested in just good food; they wanted an experience.

The owner of the bakery realized that they needed to create a brand story that would connect with their customers. They started by reflecting on what made their bakery special. They realized that their recipes had been passed down through generations and that they used only the freshest, locally-sourced ingredients.

The owner decided to create a brand story that highlighted these unique qualities. They crafted a narrative that talked about the bakery's commitment to tradition and quality. They also talked about how the bakery had been a part of the town's history for decades, and how they wanted to keep that tradition alive.

The brand story was a hit. People started coming back to the bakery, and word-of-mouth marketing began to spread. The bakery's loyal customers felt a sense of connection with the brand, and they started to share their own stories about the bakery with their friends and family.

This story highlights the importance of storytelling in branding. In today's world, customers are not just interested in buying products; they want to buy into a brand that aligns with their values and beliefs. By crafting a compelling brand story, businesses can create an emotional connection with their customers.

Here are some tips for crafting a compelling brand story:

1. Identify what makes your brand unique: Reflect on what sets your brand apart from the competition. Is it your commitment to quality, your history, or your values? Use these unique qualities to create a narrative that will resonate with your target audience.
2. Keep it simple: Your brand story should be easy to understand and remember. Focus on the key points that you want to convey and avoid jargon or complex language.
3. Be authentic: Your brand story should be true to who you are as a business. Don't try to create a story that doesn't align with your values or beliefs. Customers can quickly sense when a brand is inauthentic.

4. Make it emotional: People are more likely to remember a story that triggers an emotional response. Use storytelling techniques such as vivid imagery or relatable characters to create an emotional connection with your audience.

5. Use multiple channels to tell your story: Your brand story should be present across all channels, including your website, social media, and in-person interactions. Consistency in storytelling helps to build brand recognition and loyalty.

6. Examples of such brands are below:
Nike: Nike's brand story is centered around the idea of "just do it." This simple but powerful message has resonated with customers for decades. The brand's advertising campaigns feature athletes pushing their limits and overcoming obstacles, which inspires customers to do the same.

7. TOMS: TOMS' brand story is focused on social responsibility. The company donates a pair of shoes to a child in need for every pair of shoes sold. This story resonates with customers who want to make a positive impact on the world through their purchases.

8. Patagonia: Patagonia's brand story is all about sustainability and environmental responsibility. The company's products are made from recycled and environmentally-friendly materials, and they advocate for policies that protect the planet. This story resonates with customers who care about sustainability and want to support companies that share their values.

9. Airbnb: Airbnb's brand story is centered around the idea of "belonging anywhere." The company's advertising campaigns feature people from all over the world sharing

their experiences with the platform. This story resonates with customers who want to feel like they are part of a global community.

10. Apple: Apple's brand story is all about innovation and design. The company's products are known for their sleek and minimalist design, which sets them apart from the competition. This story resonates with customers who value quality and cutting-edge technology.

Looking for a way to craft your brand story then here are a few steps worth considering:

- Your Purpose: Start by identifying the reason your business exists beyond making money. What is your company's purpose? What impact do you want to make in the world?
- Your Unique Value Proposition: What sets your business apart from your competitors? Is it your product quality, your customer service, your values or your history?
- Your Target Audience: Who are you trying to reach with your brand story? What motivates them, what problems do they face, and what do they care about?
- Your Narrative: With the above ingredients in mind, craft a narrative that tells the story of your brand. What is the story of how your business came to be? How does your product or service make a difference in people's lives? How are you changing the world for the better?
- Your Personality: What is the tone and voice of your brand? Are you playful, serious, or irreverent? Think about the kind of personality that will resonate with your target audience.

- Your Channels: Determine the channels that will help you tell your brand story. This could be through your website, social media, advertising, events, or even packaging.
- Your Consistency: Once you have your brand story and channels established, make sure to maintain consistency in your messaging and branding. Consistency builds recognition and trust.

In conclusion, storytelling is an essential component of branding. By crafting a compelling brand story that resonates with your target audience, you can create an emotional connection with your customers, build brand loyalty, and ultimately drive business success.

5

The Role of Authenticity in Branding

Authenticity is a crucial element in branding that can help businesses build trust and loyalty with their customers. When customers perceive a brand as authentic, they are more likely to feel a genuine connection and form a long-lasting relationship with the brand. In this article, we'll explore why authenticity is important in branding, and provide guidance on how to maintain an authentic brand identity as your business evolves over time.

Why Authenticity Matters in Branding

Authenticity is important in branding because customers are increasingly looking for brands that align with their values and beliefs. When a brand is authentic, customers can trust that the company is true to its word, and that it operates with integrity. This trust can help build a loyal customer base, who will not only continue to purchase from the brand, but also recommend it to others.

In contrast, if a brand is perceived as inauthentic or disingenuous, it can quickly lose customers' trust. For example, if a brand claims to be environmentally friendly, but is found to be engaging in environmentally harmful practices, it can damage the brand's reputation and lead to a loss of customers.

Maintaining an Authentic Brand Identity

To ensure your brand remains authentic over time, it's important to regularly assess and align your brand with your values and mission. Here are some tips to help you maintain an authentic brand identity:

1. Clearly define your brand values: Your brand values should be the guiding principles that shape your business decisions and operations. Take the time to define and articulate your values, and make sure they are reflected in all aspects of your business.

2. Consistently communicate your brand message: Your brand message should be consistent across all channels and touchpoints. Use the same tone, voice, and messaging to ensure that customers have a clear understanding of what your brand stands for.

3. Be transparent: Authenticity requires transparency. Be open and honest about your business practices, and share information with customers about how your products are made, where they come from, and any potential environmental or social impact.

4. Listen to customer feedback: Listen to what your customers are saying about your brand, and use their feedback to make improvements or changes as needed. This shows that you value their opinions and are committed to providing them with the best possible experience.

5. Stay true to your values: As your business grows and

evolves, it's important to stay true to your core values. Don't compromise your values for short-term gains, as this can damage your brand's reputation in the long run.

Storytelling is an effective way to convey the importance of authenticity in branding. Through compelling stories, brands can connect with customers on a deeper level, and build trust and loyalty.

One example of a brand that has successfully used storytelling to build authentic brand identity is **Patagonia**. The outdoor clothing company has a strong commitment to environmental sustainability and ethical business practices, and it has woven these values into its brand story. For example, in its 2011 "Don't Buy This Jacket" campaign, Patagonia encouraged customers to think twice before buying new clothes and instead consider repairing or reusing the clothes they already have. The campaign was a bold move, but it reinforced the brand's values and commitment to sustainability. By telling this story, Patagonia was able to build trust and credibility with customers who share its values.

Another example of a brand that has used storytelling to create an authentic brand identity is **Airbnb**. The company has built its brand around the idea of "belonging" and creating a sense of community among its users. One way Airbnb has done this is through its "One Less Stranger" campaign, which encouraged users to perform random acts of kindness for strangers. Through this campaign, Airbnb was able to tell a compelling story that reinforced its values of community, kindness, and belonging.

In both of these examples, the brands used storytelling to reinforce their values and create an emotional connection with their customers. By telling stories that align with their values, these brands were able to build trust and authenticity, which in turn led to long-term customer loyalty.

To ensure that your brand remains authentic over time, it's important to continue to tell stories that reinforce your values and build trust with your customers. Look for opportunities to showcase your commitment to your values through your products, campaigns, and other initiatives. By staying true to your values and consistently communicating your brand message through storytelling, you can create a strong and authentic brand identity that resonates with your customers.

1. Patagonia: As mentioned earlier, Patagonia is a brand that has built its identity around environmental sustainability and ethical business practices. The company has been transparent about its supply chain and manufacturing processes and has taken bold stances on issues such as climate change and protecting public lands. By consistently communicating its values and staying true to its mission, Patagonia has built a loyal following of customers who share its values.

2. Dove: Dove has become well-known for its "Real Beauty" campaign, which celebrates diversity and challenges traditional beauty standards. The campaign has been successful in building an emotional connection with customers and has helped to establish Dove as a brand that values authenticity and inclusivity.

3. TOMS: TOMS is a shoe company that has built its brand around the concept of "One for One" - for every pair of shoes sold, the company donates a pair to someone in need. This commitment to social responsibility has resonated with customers and has helped to establish TOMS as a brand that values authenticity and making a positive impact.

4. Warby Parker: Warby Parker is a glasses and eyewear company that has built its brand around the concept of "disrupting" the eyewear industry by offering affordable, high-quality glasses directly to consumers. The company has been transparent about its supply chain and pricing and has worked to establish a strong emotional connection with its customers through storytelling and social responsibility initiatives.

In conclusion, authenticity is a critical component of branding that can help businesses build trust and loyalty with their customers. By clearly defining your brand values, consistently communicating your brand message, being transparent, listening to customer feedback, and staying true to your values, you can maintain an authentic brand identity that resonates with customers and sets your business up for long-term success.

6

Conducting Market Research: Understanding Your Audience and Competition

Market research is a critical component of any branding strategy. It helps businesses to understand their target audience, identify their needs and preferences, and assess their competition. By conducting market research, businesses can make informed decisions about their branding and marketing efforts, ensuring that they resonate with their audience and stand out from the competition.

To conduct market research, start by analyzing customer data. This can include information such as demographic data, purchase history, and online behavior. By studying this data, businesses can gain insights into their customers' interests and behavior patterns, allowing them to tailor their branding efforts to better meet their needs.

Another key component of market research is studying the

competition. This involves analyzing their branding, marketing campaigns, and product offerings. By understanding what sets their competition apart, businesses can identify opportunities to differentiate themselves and create a unique value proposition.

To conduct a competitive analysis, start by identifying your key competitors. This can be done by conducting online research, reviewing industry publications, and attending industry events. Once you have identified your competitors, analyze their branding, marketing campaigns, and product offerings. Identify what makes them unique, and look for areas where you can differentiate yourself.

In addition to analyzing customer data and studying the competition, businesses can also conduct market research through surveys, focus groups, and other research methods. Surveys can provide valuable insights into customer preferences and behavior, while focus groups can provide in-depth feedback on specific products or services.

Ultimately, conducting market research is essential for businesses looking to build a strong brand and stand out in a crowded marketplace. By understanding their audience and competition, businesses can make informed decisions about their branding and marketing efforts, creating a unique value proposition that resonates with their target market.

Explanation in the form of a story:
Meet John, a budding entrepreneur who dreams of starting his own e-commerce store. John has been working hard to

develop his product line, perfect his website, and set up his social media accounts. He is excited to launch his business and start selling his products to customers all over the world.

However, before John launches his e-commerce store, he realizes that he needs to conduct market research to better understand his target audience and competition. He knows that by doing so, he can make informed branding decisions that will help him stand out in a crowded marketplace.

John begins by analyzing customer data. He uses online tools to study his target audience's demographics, preferences, and online behavior. He discovers that his audience is primarily made up of tech-savvy millennials who value sustainable and ethical products. Armed with this information, John can tailor his branding efforts to better meet his customers' needs and preferences.

Next, John studies his competition. He spends hours re-searching his competitors' branding, marketing campaigns, and product offerings. He discovers that while his competitors offer similar products, they all have different value proposi-tions. Some focus on sustainability, while others focus on affordability. John identifies an opportunity to differentiate himself by focusing on quality and customer service, knowing that his target audience values these attributes.

To further his market research efforts, John also conducts surveys and focus groups to gain insights into his customers' preferences and behavior. He learns that his customers value convenience, fast shipping, and a hassle-free return policy.

With his market research complete, John is now ready to launch his e-commerce store. He has a better understanding of his target audience, competition, and what sets his business apart. He uses this information to develop a strong brand identity that resonates with his customers and stands out in a crowded marketplace.

Thanks to his market research efforts, John's e-commerce store is a success. His customers appreciate the quality of his products, his commitment to sustainability, and his excellent customer service. John knows that conducting market research was essential to his success and will continue to use it to inform his branding decisions and stay ahead of the competition.

Some examples of brands that used market research:

1. Coca-Cola - In the 1980s, Coca-Cola conducted market research that revealed consumers preferred the taste of Pepsi in blind taste tests. As a result, Coca-Cola launched "New Coke" with a sweeter taste to try to compete with Pepsi. However, this move proved unpopular, and after months of backlash, Coca-Cola brought back the original formula as "Coca-Cola Classic." This market research helped Coca-Cola understand the importance of brand loyalty and the emotional connection consumers have with their products, leading to the company's continued success today.

2. Amazon - Amazon's success is largely due to its commitment to customer-centricity, which is rooted in extensive market research. Amazon's founder, Jeff Bezos, famously said, "We're not competitor obsessed, we're customer ob-

sessed. We start with the customer and work backwards."
By studying customer data and behavior, Amazon has
been able to develop personalized recommendations, fast
and reliable shipping options, and a user-friendly website
that has made it one of the most successful e-commerce
companies in the world.

3. Airbnb - Airbnb's success can be attributed in part to
   its market research efforts. The company conducted
   extensive research on consumer behavior and preferences,
   which led to the development of a platform that emphasized the importance of unique and personalized travel
   experiences. This approach helped Airbnb differentiate
   itself from traditional hotel chains and has contributed to
   the company's rapid growth and success.

4. Apple - Apple has built its success on a deep understanding
   of its target audience's preferences and behavior. The
   company's market research has helped it develop products
   that are both functional and aesthetically pleasing, with an
   emphasis on design and user experience. This approach
   has helped Apple develop a loyal customer base and
   become one of the most valuable brands in the world.

7

Creating a Brand Strategy: Setting Goals and Objectives

Creating a Brand Strategy: Setting Goals and Objectives

In today's competitive business environment, a strong brand is critical for success. A well-defined brand strategy can guide your branding decisions and help you stand out from the crowd. A brand strategy sets the foundation for all aspects of your branding, including your brand identity, messaging, and marketing efforts. In this article, we'll discuss the importance of a brand strategy and provide guidance on how to create one, including setting goals and objectives.

Importance of a Brand Strategy

A brand strategy is a long-term plan for building and managing your brand. It encompasses everything from your brand identity and messaging to your marketing and communication efforts. A well-executed brand strategy can help you differentiate yourself from competitors, attract and retain customers, and build brand loyalty.

Your brand strategy should be informed by market research, customer insights, and an understanding of your competitive landscape. It should also align with your overall business goals and objectives. A strong brand strategy can help you achieve these goals by providing a clear roadmap for your branding efforts.

How to Create a Brand Strategy

Creating a brand strategy can seem like a daunting task, but it doesn't have to be. The key is to approach it systematically, starting with your goals and objectives. Here's a step-by-step guide to creating a brand strategy:

Step 1: Define Your Goals and Objectives

The first step in creating a brand strategy is to define your goals and objectives. What do you want your brand to achieve? Do you want to increase brand awareness, drive sales, or build brand loyalty? Your goals and objectives should be specific, measurable, achievable, relevant, and time-bound (SMART).

Step 2: Conduct Market Research

Once you've defined your goals and objectives, you need to conduct market research to gain a deeper understanding of your target audience, competitive landscape, and market trends. This research can include surveys, focus groups, and social media listening.

Step 3: Define Your Brand Identity

Your brand identity is the visual and verbal representation of your brand. It includes your brand name, logo, colors, typography, and messaging. Define your brand identity based

33

on your target audience and competitive landscape.

Step 4: Develop Your Brand Messaging

Your brand messaging is the language and tone you use to communicate your brand's values, personality, and benefits to your target audience. It should be consistent across all marketing channels and aligned with your brand identity.

Step 5: Create a Brand Marketing Plan

Your brand marketing plan outlines the tactics you'll use to reach your target audience and achieve your branding goals. It should include a mix of traditional and digital marketing channels, such as advertising, social media, content marketing, and public relations.

Step 6: Monitor and Measure Your Brand's Performance

Finally, it's important to monitor and measure your brand's performance over time to ensure that your branding efforts are effective. Use tools like Google Analytics and social media analytics to track your brand's reach, engagement, and conversions.

Explanation in the form of a story:

Meet Alice, a small business owner who runs a bakery. Alice loves baking and has a passion for creating delicious treats, but she's struggling to stand out in a crowded market. She's tried various marketing tactics, but nothing seems to be working.

One day, Alice attends a business conference and hears a speaker talking about the importance of a brand strategy. The speaker explains that a strong brand strategy can guide your branding decisions and help you stand out from the crowd. Intrigued, Alice decides to learn more about creating a brand strategy for her bakery.

Alice starts by defining her goals and objectives. She wants to increase brand awareness and drive sales, but she's not sure how to achieve these goals. She decides to conduct market research to gain a deeper understanding of her target audience, competitive landscape, and market trends.

Through her research, Alice discovers that her target audience is mostly young adults who are health-conscious and interested in organic, gluten-free, and vegan options. She also learns that there are several other bakeries in her area that offer similar products.

Armed with this information, Alice defines her brand identity based on her target audience and competitive landscape. She creates a new logo and brand colors that reflect her bakery's values and personality.

Next, Alice develops her brand messaging. She decides to focus on the quality and freshness of her ingredients, as well as her bakery's commitment to sustainability and community involvement. She creates a tagline that sums up her brand's values: "Freshly baked with love, for you and the planet."

Alice then creates a brand marketing plan that includes a mix of traditional and digital marketing channels. She decides to run ads in local newspapers and magazines, launch a social media campaign, and offer promotions for first-time customers.

Alice monitors and measures her brand's performance over time to ensure that her branding efforts are effective. She uses tools like Google Analytics and social media analytics to track her brand's reach, engagement, and conversions. She adjusts her marketing tactics as needed based on the data.

Thanks to her brand strategy, Alice's bakery starts to stand out from the competition. Customers appreciate her bakery's commitment to quality ingredients, sustainability, and community involvement. Her sales increase, and her brand awareness grows.

In the end, Alice realizes that a strong brand strategy can make all the difference in the success of her business. By defining her goals and objectives, conducting market research, and creating a brand identity and messaging that resonates with her target audience, she was able to build a strong brand for her bakery.

Conclusion

A strong brand strategy is essential for building a successful brand. It can guide your branding decisions and help you stand out from the crowd. When creating a brand strategy, start by defining your goals and objectives, conduct market research, define your brand identity, develop your brand messaging, create a brand marketing plan, and monitor and measure your brand's performance. By following these steps, you can create a brand strategy that will help you achieve your branding goals and build a strong brand for your business.

8

Designing Your Brand Visuals: Logos, Colors, and Typography

Brand visuals are a crucial component of any business's marketing strategy. A strong visual identity can differentiate a company from its competitors, communicate its values and mission, and help create a memorable brand that resonates with customers. In this article, we'll discuss the importance of brand visuals and provide guidance on how to design a strong visual identity for your brand, including selecting colors, typography, and creating a logo.

Why are brand visuals important?

Brand visuals are critical in creating a strong brand identity. They are the first thing that people see when they encounter your brand, and they communicate the tone, personality, and values of your business. If your visuals are poorly designed or inconsistent, you risk confusing or alienating potential customers. On the other hand, a cohesive and visually appealing brand identity can help build trust, inspire loyalty, and differentiate your brand from competitors.

Selecting colors

When selecting colors for your brand, it's essential to consider the psychology behind them. Different colors evoke different emotions and associations, so it's important to choose colors that align with your brand's values and personality. For example, blue is often associated with trust, reliability, and professionalism, making it a popular choice for financial and tech companies. In contrast, red is associated with excitement, passion, and energy, making it a popular choice for brands that want to convey a sense of urgency or excitement.

Typography

Typography refers to the style and arrangement of letters and characters. Choosing the right typography for your brand can help communicate its personality and values. When selecting typography, it's important to consider legibility, hierarchy, and style. Your typography should be easy to read and distinguishable at different sizes, and it should be arranged in a way that guides the reader's eye through the content. You should also consider the style of the typography, as different styles can convey different emotions and associations. For example, sans-serif fonts are often associated with modernity and simplicity, while serif fonts are often associated with tradition and sophistication.

Creating a logo

Your logo is one of the most important components of your brand's visual identity. It's often the first thing people see when they encounter your brand, and it should be memorable, distinctive, and reflective of your brand's personality and values. When designing a logo, it's important to consider the following:

- Simplicity: Your logo should be easy to recognize and remember, even when viewed in small sizes.
- Distinctiveness: Your logo should be unique and different from competitors to help your brand stand out.
- Relevance: Your logo should reflect your brand's personality, values, and mission.
- Versatility: Your logo should be adaptable to different formats and contexts, such as social media profiles, business cards, and signage.

Explanation in the form of a story:

Once upon a time, there was a small coffee shop located in the heart of a bustling city. The owner of the coffee shop, a young entrepreneur named Sarah, had a passion for coffee and wanted to share her love for it with the world. However, despite her delicious coffee and friendly service, Sarah struggled to attract and retain customers.

One day, Sarah met a branding expert named Emma, who had a reputation for helping small businesses like hers establish a strong visual identity. Emma explained to Sarah the importance of brand visuals in creating a memorable and distinctive brand, and how it can help differentiate her business from competitors.

Emma worked with Sarah to design a new visual identity for

her coffee shop. They started by selecting colors that would reflect the warmth and coziness of the shop. They chose a warm shade of brown for the main color, which was inspired by the color of coffee beans, and paired it with a soft shade of cream for a calming effect.

Next, they worked on typography. Emma suggested a modern sans-serif font for the logo and menu, which would give a contemporary and approachable feel to the brand. She also suggested using a handwritten font for the specials board, which would add a personal touch and a sense of authenticity.

Finally, they worked on creating a logo. Emma took inspiration from the coffee shop's location, which was situated next to a small park. She came up with a simple yet distinctive logo featuring a coffee cup surrounded by leaves, which would reflect the coffee shop's commitment to using organic and locally sourced ingredients.

After implementing the new visual identity, Sarah noticed an immediate difference in the number of customers visiting her coffee shop. They commented on how warm and inviting the shop felt, and how the new visuals reflected the quality and care that went into each cup of coffee.

As time went by, Sarah's coffee shop became a staple in the community, and her loyal customers praised her for her dedication to quality and authenticity. Thanks to Emma's expertise in branding, Sarah was able to create a memorable and distinctive visual identity that set her apart from competitors and resonated with customers.

Conclusion

Designing a strong visual identity for your brand is essential in creating a memorable and distinctive brand that resonates with customers. By selecting colors, typography, and creating a logo that aligns with your brand's personality and values, you can differentiate your brand from competitors, build trust, and inspire loyalty. Remember, consistency is key, so make sure your visual identity is applied consistently across all your marketing channels and touchpoints.

9

Building a Consistent Brand Voice: Tone, Language, and Messaging

In today's competitive market, building a consistent brand voice is vital to creating a recognizable brand and a strong connection with your target audience. A consistent brand voice is a key element of branding, which helps businesses create a unique identity and differentiate themselves from their competitors. In this context, a brand voice refers to the way a business communicates with its audience through the tone, language, and messaging used in all forms of communication, such as marketing materials, social media posts, and customer interactions.

A consistent brand voice helps build brand recognition by creating a consistent experience for the audience. When the audience encounters your brand in different places, such as on your website, social media, or advertising, they should be able to recognize your brand's voice and feel a sense of familiarity. This consistency creates trust and builds a stronger relationship with the audience. When customers feel like they know a brand well, they are more likely to become loyal and advocate for the brand, recommending it to others.

To develop a consistent brand voice, businesses need to consider their target audience, brand personality, and company values. It's important to determine the tone, language, and messaging that will best resonate with the audience and convey the desired brand personality. Here are some guidelines for developing a consistent brand voice:

1. Determine the tone: The tone should match the brand's personality and values. Consider whether the brand should be serious, playful, witty, or authoritative. The tone should also reflect the target audience's preferences and expectations.
2. Choose the language: The language used should match the tone and be appropriate for the audience. For example, a brand targeting a younger audience may use more casual language and slang than a brand targeting older audiences.
3. Define the messaging: The messaging should be consistent across all communication channels and reflect the brand's core values and mission. This includes key messages, taglines, and unique selling propositions.
4. Train employees: Consistency in brand voice requires that all employees understand the brand voice and messaging. Train employees to communicate consistently, whether they're in customer service, sales, or marketing.
5. Monitor and adjust: Regularly monitor the brand's communication channels to ensure consistency and adjust the brand voice as necessary to stay relevant and connected to the audience.

Explanation in the form of a story:

Once upon a time, there was a small business owner named Lily. Lily had a passion for creating delicious baked goods and wanted to share her love of baking with the world. She decided to start her own bakery and called it "Lily's Sweets."

Lily knew that in order to make her bakery successful, she needed to create a brand that people could easily recognize and trust. She decided to focus on building a consistent brand voice, which would help her connect with her customers and create a strong sense of loyalty.

To develop a consistent brand voice, Lily first needed to consider her target audience. She wanted to appeal to people who appreciated high-quality baked goods and valued natural ingredients. She decided to use a warm and friendly tone in her communications, which would make people feel welcome and comfortable in her bakery.

Next, Lily chose the language that would best suit her brand's personality. She knew that her customers appreciated the art of baking, so she used words like "artisanal" and "hand-crafted" to describe her products. She also made sure to use simple and easy-to-understand language, so that everyone could appreciate and understand her passion for baking.

Finally, Lily developed messaging that would convey her bakery's values and mission. She focused on creating a message of authenticity and quality, emphasizing that all of her baked goods were made with natural ingredients and without any artificial preservatives.

As Lily's bakery grew, she made sure to train her employees to communicate consistently with the brand voice she had developed. She also monitored her communication channels regularly to ensure that her bakery's messaging remained consistent and aligned with her brand's values.

Thanks to Lily's consistent brand voice, her bakery quickly became a beloved neighborhood spot. People would often stop by just to say hello and catch up on the latest news, all while enjoying a delicious pastry or cookie. And Lily's Sweets continued to thrive, thanks to the strong connection she had built with her customers through her warm and friendly brand voice.

Quick example:

1. Apple: Apple is a great example of a brand with a consistent brand voice. From their marketing materials to their customer service interactions, Apple's tone is always confident, minimalist, and focused on innovation.
2. Nike: Nike is known for its inspiring and motivational brand voice, which is consistent across all of its communication channels. Their messaging focuses on empowering athletes and encouraging people to push themselves to be their best.
3. Airbnb: Airbnb has a warm and welcoming brand voice that makes people feel at home. Their language is simple and friendly, and their messaging focuses on creating meaningful travel experiences for their guests.
4. Coca-Cola: Coca-Cola's brand voice is consistently cheerful and optimistic. Their messaging focuses on spreading happiness and sharing special moments with loved ones, which is reflected in their advertising campaigns and social media content.
5. Patagonia: Patagonia is known for its authentic and

environmentally conscious brand voice. Their messaging focuses on sustainability and social responsibility, which is reflected in their product design and marketing materials.

In summary, a consistent brand voice is crucial to building brand recognition and a strong relationship with the audience. By determining the tone, language, and messaging that reflect the brand's personality and values, businesses can develop a consistent brand voice that resonates with the target audience and sets them apart from the competition.

10

Branding Across Platforms: Social Media, Websites, and Marketing Materials

Branding Across Platforms: Social Media, Websites, and Marketing Materials

Branding is a critical aspect of a company's success. It involves creating a unique identity that differentiates a business from its competitors and resonates with its target audience. To build a strong brand, it is essential to maintain consistency across all platforms and touchpoints, including social media, websites, and marketing materials. In this article, we will discuss the importance of consistency in branding across these platforms and provide guidance on how to ensure your branding remains consistent.

Importance of Consistency in Branding Across Platforms and Touchpoints

Builds Trust and Recognition: Consistency in branding helps build trust and recognition with your target audience. When people see consistent branding across various touchpoints, they are more likely to remember your brand and trust it.

Establishes a Strong Brand Image: A consistent brand image across platforms and touchpoints strengthens your brand's identity and helps you establish a unique brand image. This creates a memorable brand that resonates with your target audience and sets you apart from competitors.

Boosts Credibility: Consistent branding across platforms and touchpoints helps build credibility with your target audience. It shows that your business is professional, reliable, and trustworthy.

Guidance on Ensuring Consistency in Branding

Develop Brand Guidelines: The first step in ensuring consistency in branding is to create brand guidelines. These guidelines should include your brand's visual identity, tone of voice, messaging, and brand values. These guidelines provide a framework for all branding efforts across platforms and touchpoints.

Use Consistent Visual Elements: Consistency in visual elements such as color schemes, typography, logos, and imagery helps create a cohesive brand identity. Use the same visual elements across social media, websites, and marketing materials to maintain brand consistency.

Maintain Consistent Tone of Voice: The tone of voice used in your brand messaging is also important in maintaining consistency. Use the same tone of voice across all platforms and touchpoints to ensure your brand's personality and voice are consistent.

Monitor Your Brand Across Platforms: Monitoring your brand across platforms is critical to ensure consistency. Check that your branding is consistent on all platforms, including social media, websites, and marketing materials.

Train Your Team: Train your team on the importance of consistency in branding and ensure they follow the brand guidelines when creating content across platforms and touchpoints.

Explanation in the form of a story:

Once upon a time, there was a small clothing brand that had just started its business. The owner of the brand, Anna, wanted to make sure that her brand stood out from the competition and resonated with her target audience.

Anna knew that consistency in branding was essential to build trust and recognition with her target audience. She decided to create a unique brand identity that was consistent across all platforms and touchpoints, including social media, websites, and marketing materials.

Anna began by developing brand guidelines that included her brand's visual identity, tone of voice, messaging, and brand values. She wanted to ensure that her brand's personality and voice were consistent, no matter where her target audience encountered her brand.

Next, Anna focused on maintaining consistency in visual el-

49

ements such as color schemes, typography, logos, and imagery. She used the same visual elements across all platforms and touchpoints to create a cohesive brand identity that resonated with her target audience.

Anna also monitored her brand across platforms to ensure consistency. She checked that her branding was consistent on all platforms, including social media, websites, and marketing materials. This helped her ensure that her target audience saw a consistent brand image no matter where they encountered her brand.

Anna trained her team on the importance of consistency in branding and ensured they followed the brand guidelines when creating content across platforms and touchpoints. This helped her team understand the importance of consistency in branding and helped maintain consistency in her brand's messaging.

As a result of Anna's efforts, her small clothing brand grew rapidly. Her target audience resonated with her brand's unique identity, and her business became a recognizable and memorable brand in the fashion industry.

In conclusion, Anna's story illustrates the importance of consistency in branding across platforms and touchpoints. By creating a unique brand identity and maintaining consistency in visual elements and tone of voice, monitoring her brand across platforms, and training her team on the importance of consistency in branding, Anna built a successful business that resonated with her target audience.

Quick example of brands who implemented similar thoughts:

1. Apple - Apple is a prime example of a brand that has consistently maintained its brand image across all platforms and touchpoints. The company's visual identity, tone of voice, and messaging are consistent across its products, packaging, advertising, and social media channels.

2. Coca-Cola - Coca-Cola has been successful in maintaining a consistent brand identity across multiple touchpoints. The company's iconic red and white color scheme, logo, and brand messaging have remained consistent for over a century, and the company has maintained this consistency across its products, packaging, advertising, and social media channels.

3. Nike - Nike has a strong and consistent brand image across multiple platforms and touchpoints. The company's visual identity, tone of voice, and messaging are consistent across its products, packaging, advertising, and social media channels. Nike's iconic "Just Do It" tagline and the Swoosh logo are instantly recognizable, and the company has successfully maintained this consistency for several decades.

4. Airbnb - Airbnb has built a strong and consistent brand image across multiple touchpoints. The company's visual identity, tone of voice, and messaging are consistent across its website, mobile app, advertising, and social media channels. Airbnb's brand personality and voice are consistent, and the company's messaging focuses on providing unique and authentic travel experiences.

5. Tesla - Tesla has created a unique and consistent brand image across multiple touchpoints. The company's visual identity, tone of voice, and messaging are consistent across its products, packaging, advertising, and social media

channels. Tesla's brand messaging focuses on innovation, sustainability, and the future, and the company has successfully maintained this consistency since its inception.

Conclusion

Consistency in branding is crucial for building a strong brand that resonates with your target audience. Maintaining consistency across social media, websites, and marketing materials helps build trust and recognition, establishes a strong brand image, and boosts credibility. To ensure consistency in branding, develop brand guidelines, use consistent visual elements and tone of voice, monitor your brand across platforms, and train your team on the importance of consistency in branding. By following these guidelines, you can create a memorable and recognizable brand that sets you apart from competitors.

11

Developing Your Brand Guidelines: How to Ensure Consistency

Developing Your Brand Guidelines: How to Ensure Consistency

In the modern business world, brand identity is one of the most critical aspects of any company's success. A well-defined brand can help a business stand out from the competition, establish customer loyalty, and create a lasting impression on the minds of potential customers. However, building a strong brand is not a one-time effort; it requires consistent and cohesive branding decisions across all aspects of a business's operations. This is where brand guidelines come in.

Brand guidelines are a set of rules and standards that define how a company should represent itself visually and tonally to its customers. They provide a roadmap for employees and partners to follow when creating marketing materials, messaging, and other brand-related assets. A well-crafted set of brand guidelines can ensure consistency in branding decisions and protect a company's brand equity. In this article, we will discuss the importance of brand guidelines and provide guidance on how to develop comprehensive brand guidelines that cover all aspects of branding.

Importance of Brand Guidelines

The benefits of having a comprehensive set of brand guidelines are numerous. They include:

1. Consistency: Brand guidelines ensure that all branding decisions are consistent across all mediums, from print to digital media.
2. Brand Recognition: Clear and consistent branding helps customers recognize a company and differentiate it from competitors.
3. Trust: Consistent branding builds trust with customers, as they come to associate a particular brand with quality, reliability, and authenticity.
4. Efficiency: Having a set of guidelines ensures that marketing materials can be created efficiently and quickly, without the need for constant revisions.
5. Protection: Guidelines protect a company's brand equity by ensuring that branding decisions are consistent and aligned with the company's values and mission.

Developing Comprehensive Brand Guidelines

To develop a comprehensive set of brand guidelines, a company should consider the following steps:

1. Define Brand Identity: Define the company's vision, mission, and values. Develop a clear understanding of the brand's personality, tone, and voice. This information

will form the foundation of the brand guidelines.

2. Establish Visual Identity: Define the visual identity of the brand, including logo, color palette, typography, and imagery. Provide guidance on how these elements should be used in different mediums, such as print, web, and social media.

3. Define Messaging Guidelines: Establish messaging guidelines for all forms of communication, including social media, advertising, public relations, and internal communications. Guidelines should cover tone of voice, language, and messaging themes.

4. Consider Brand Applications: Consider all the different applications of the brand, from business cards to product packaging. Develop guidelines that cover all applications and ensure consistency across them.

5. Outline Brand Management: Establish guidelines for managing the brand, including how to handle brand extensions, partnerships, and collaborations. Include guidelines for monitoring and enforcing brand standards.

6. Collaborate and Test: Involve stakeholders, partners, and employees in the development process to ensure that guidelines are practical and applicable. Test guidelines in different mediums to ensure that they work in practice.

Explanation in the form of a story:

Once upon a time, there was a small business owner named Lily. She owned a boutique clothing store that sold unique and fashionable clothing for women. Lily was passionate about her business and worked hard to make it a success. She spent long hours designing her clothes, selecting the best materials, and coming up with creative marketing strategies to promote her business.

However, Lily soon realized that her branding was inconsistent. Her store's logo, social media posts, and promotional materials had different colors, fonts, and imagery. This inconsistency made it hard for customers to recognize her brand, and it confused them about what her business stood for. As a result, Lily's sales were not growing as she had hoped, and she was losing customers to her competitors.

Lily knew she had to do something about it. She decided to create a set of brand guidelines that would help her maintain consistency across all aspects of her business's branding. She began by defining her brand identity, vision, mission, and values. She wanted her brand to stand for creativity, uniqueness, and empowerment of women.

Next, she worked on creating a visual identity for her brand. She selected a color palette that reflected her brand's personality, and designed a logo that would be used across all her branding materials. She chose a unique and trendy font that would be used in all her communications.

Lily then defined messaging guidelines for her brand. She decided on a tone of voice that was friendly, approachable, and empowering. She crafted messaging themes that would resonate with her target audience, such as "Be unique, be yourself."

She also considered all the different applications of her brand, from store signage to product packaging. She developed guidelines that would ensure consistency across all mediums.

Finally, Lily outlined a plan for brand management, including how to handle collaborations and partnerships. She made sure that all her employees and partners understood the brand guidelines and were on board with implementing them.

The result of Lily's hard work was a set of brand guidelines that brought consistency and coherence to her branding decisions. Her store's logo, social media posts, and promotional materials all had the same colors, fonts, and imagery. Her customers could easily recognize her brand, and they knew what it stood for. Lily's business began to grow, and she attracted new customers who were drawn to her brand's unique identity.

In the end, Lily realized that developing a set of brand guidelines was essential for her business's success. By creating a consistent and recognizable brand identity, she was able to establish trust with her customers and differentiate her business from her competitors. She was proud of her brand, and her customers were proud to wear her clothes.

Conclusion

In conclusion, a comprehensive set of brand guidelines is essential for establishing and maintaining a strong brand identity. Guidelines ensure consistency across all aspects of a company's operations and protect the brand's equity. To develop a set of brand guidelines, a company should define its brand identity, establish a visual identity, define messaging guidelines, consider brand applications, outline brand management, and collaborate and test with stakeholders. By following these steps, a company can develop a set of guidelines that will help it establish a strong and consistent brand identity.

12

Building Your Brand Reputation: Creating a Positive Image

Building Your Brand Reputation: Creating a Positive Image

In today's competitive business environment, building a strong brand reputation is crucial for the success of any business. A brand reputation refers to the way a company is perceived by its target audience, stakeholders, and the wider community. A positive brand reputation can help businesses stand out from their competitors, increase customer loyalty, and attract new customers. On the other hand, a negative brand reputation can harm a business's image, reduce customer trust, and even lead to a decline in sales.

Here are some reasons why building a strong brand reputation is essential for business success:

1. Differentiation: A strong brand reputation can help businesses differentiate themselves from their competi-

58

tors by highlighting their unique value proposition and establishing their brand identity.

2. Trust and Credibility: A positive brand reputation can build trust and credibility with customers, making them more likely to choose your business over competitors.

3. Customer Loyalty: A positive brand reputation can increase customer loyalty, encouraging repeat business and referrals.

4. Financial Performance: A strong brand reputation can positively impact a business's financial performance by increasing sales, improving margins, and attracting investors.

Now, let's look at some ways to build a positive brand image:

1. Provide Excellent Customer Service: Delivering exceptional customer service is one of the best ways to build a positive brand reputation. Responding to customer inquiries promptly and effectively, and providing personalized experiences can enhance customer satisfaction, loyalty, and advocacy.

2. Create Valuable Content: Creating valuable content can help build a positive brand image by demonstrating expertise, providing insights, and solving customers' problems. Useful content can also attract new customers and increase brand visibility.

3. Engage with Customers: Engaging with customers through social media, email, or other communication channels can help build relationships and enhance brand loyalty. Responding to customer feedback and

addressing their concerns can demonstrate a commitment to customer satisfaction and build trust.

4. Manage Online Reviews: Online reviews can significantly impact a business's reputation. Responding to both positive and negative reviews in a professional and empathetic manner can show customers that the business values their feedback and is committed to improving their experience.

Explanation in the form of a story:

Once upon a time, there was a small bakery called Sweet Delights. The owner, Maria, was passionate about baking and had been running the bakery for five years. She had a loyal customer base, but she wanted to expand her business and attract new customers.

Maria knew that the bakery's reputation was critical to achieving her goal, so she focused on building a positive brand image. She started by providing exceptional customer service, greeting every customer with a warm smile and a friendly welcome. She listened carefully to their needs and offered personalized recommendations.

Maria also created valuable content by sharing recipes, baking tips, and behind-the-scenes footage of the bakery on social media. Her content attracted new customers who were impressed by the bakery's expertise and quality.

To engage with customers, Maria launched a loyalty program that rewarded customers with discounts and exclusive offers. She also started a blog where customers could share their experiences and provide feedback. She responded to every comment and showed customers that their opinions mattered.

Maria knew that online reviews were critical to building a strong brand reputation, so she actively managed them.

She responded to both positive and negative reviews and addressed any issues that customers had raised. Her prompt and professional responses demonstrated a commitment to customer satisfaction and showed potential customers that the bakery cared about its customers.

Thanks to Maria's efforts, Sweet Delights' brand reputation grew, and the bakery became a popular destination for locals and tourists alike. Maria's focus on providing exceptional customer service, creating valuable content, engaging with customers, and managing online reviews had paid off. Sweet Delights had established a positive brand reputation, which had differentiated it from competitors, built trust and credibility with customers, and increased customer loyalty and advocacy.

The moral of the story is that building a strong brand reputation is essential for business success. By following Maria's example and focusing on delivering excellent customer service, creating valuable content, engaging with customers, and managing online reviews, businesses can establish a positive brand reputation that sets them apart from competitors, builds customer loyalty, and attracts new customers.

Quick examples:

1. Apple - Apple is a company that has built a strong brand reputation over the years. It has established itself as a leader in the technology industry by providing innovative and high-quality products, such as the iPhone and MacBook. Apple's brand reputation is based on its commitment to customer satisfaction, simplicity, and design.
2. Amazon - Amazon is another company that has built

a strong brand reputation. It has become the go-to online retailer for millions of customers around the world. Amazon's brand reputation is based on its exceptional customer service, fast delivery, and broad selection of products.

3. Nike - Nike is a company that has built a strong brand reputation in the sportswear industry. Its brand reputation is based on its commitment to high-quality products, innovation, and celebrity endorsements. Nike's "Just Do It" slogan has become iconic, and it has positioned itself as a brand that inspires people to achieve their goals.

4. Zappos - Zappos is an online shoe and clothing retailer that has built a strong brand reputation by providing exceptional customer service. Its brand reputation is based on its commitment to customer satisfaction, including its 365-day return policy and free shipping. Zappos has also built a reputation for being a fun and quirky company, with a strong culture that values its employees.

5. Patagonia - Patagonia is a company that has built a strong brand reputation in the outdoor apparel industry. Its brand reputation is based on its commitment to sustainability, environmental responsibility, and ethical business practices. Patagonia has also built a reputation for quality, innovation, and durability, with products that are designed to last.

In conclusion, building a strong brand reputation is crucial for business success. By providing excellent customer service, creating valuable content, engaging with customers, and managing online reviews, businesses can build a positive brand image that can differentiate them from competitors, build trust and credibility, and increase customer loyalty and advocacy.

13

Crisis Management: Protecting Your Brand in Times of Trouble

Crisis management is a process that helps companies prepare for and respond to unexpected events that can harm their brand reputation, business operations, and financial performance. Effective crisis management is critical for protecting a brand's reputation and maintaining customer trust and loyalty.

The importance of crisis management lies in its ability to help organizations anticipate, prevent, and manage crises that can negatively impact their brand. Crises can come in various forms, such as natural disasters, product recalls, data breaches, or reputational crises caused by negative media coverage or social media backlash. These events can cause significant damage to a company's brand reputation, credibility, and financial performance, making it essential for companies to be prepared to respond quickly and effectively.

When a crisis strikes, the speed and effectiveness of a company's response can make a significant difference in how well it manages the situation and protects its brand reputation. Failing to address the issue quickly and transparently can result in long-term damage to a brand's image and customer trust, and potentially lead to lost revenue and market share.

To protect their brand reputation during a crisis, companies must have a comprehensive crisis management plan in place. A crisis management plan outlines the steps and procedures that a company will take to manage a crisis and communicate effectively with customers, stakeholders, and the media.

The following are some key steps to consider when developing a crisis management plan:

1. Identify potential risks and scenarios that could impact your brand: Conduct a risk assessment to identify potential crises that could impact your business, and develop a plan for addressing each scenario.
2. Establish a crisis management team: Identify key members of your team who will be responsible for managing a crisis and responding to customer inquiries.
3. Develop a crisis communication plan: Develop a plan for communicating with customers, stakeholders, and the media during a crisis, including messaging and communication channels.
4. Train your team: Ensure that your team is trained to respond quickly and effectively to a crisis and is familiar with the crisis management plan.
5. Monitor and assess the situation: Stay informed about the situation, and continuously assess the impact on your business and brand reputation.

6. Take action: Act quickly to address the crisis and minimize the impact on your brand and business operations.

7. Review and learn: After the crisis has been resolved, review the response and learn from the experience to improve future crisis management efforts.

Effective communication is a critical component of crisis management. During a crisis, companies must communicate openly, honestly, and transparently with customers, stakeholders, and the media. They must provide accurate information, be responsive to inquiries, and demonstrate empathy and concern for those affected by the crisis.

To communicate effectively during a crisis, companies should consider the following:

1. Be proactive: Be the first to communicate with customers and stakeholders about the situation and what steps you are taking to address it.

2. Be transparent: Share accurate and timely information about the crisis and its impact on your business, and provide updates as the situation evolves.

3. Show empathy: Demonstrate concern for those affected by the crisis, and provide resources and support as needed.

4. Use appropriate communication channels: Use the channels that your customers and stakeholders are most likely to use to receive information about the crisis.

Explanation in the form of a story:

Once upon a time, there was a successful clothing company that had been in business for many years. The company had a good reputation for producing high-quality, fashionable clothing and had a loyal customer base. However, one day, the company faced a crisis that threatened to damage its brand reputation and financial performance.

The crisis began when a customer posted on social media that they had found a piece of metal in one of the company's shirts. The post went viral, and soon other customers started sharing their own experiences of finding foreign objects in their clothing. The company immediately began receiving negative comments and feedback on social media and other online platforms, and sales started to decline.

The company's management team quickly realized that they needed to take action to address the crisis and protect their brand reputation. They assembled a crisis management team and began working on a plan to address the issue.

The first step the company took was to investigate the source of the problem. They discovered that the issue was caused by a faulty machine in one of their manufacturing facilities, which was causing small metal parts to come loose and get mixed in with the clothing during production.

The company then developed a crisis communication plan to address the issue. They immediately issued a public apology, explaining what had happened and what steps they were taking to address the issue. They also offered refunds to customers who had purchased affected clothing items and promised to improve their manufacturing processes to prevent similar incidents from happening in the future.

The company also made sure to communicate regularly with customers, stakeholders, and the media throughout the crisis. They provided updates on the progress of their investigation and efforts to fix the issue, and they were transparent about the steps they were taking to ensure the safety and quality of their clothing.

Through their proactive and transparent communication, the company was able to restore customer trust and confidence in their brand. Sales gradually started to recover, and the company emerged from the crisis with its reputation intact.

The company learned an important lesson from the crisis and decided to implement changes to their crisis management plan. They increased the frequency of their quality checks and implemented new measures to ensure the safety and quality of their clothing. They also increased their social media monitoring efforts to respond quickly to any future issues that may arise.

In the end, the company's quick and effective crisis management response helped to protect their brand reputation and maintain customer loyalty. The experience taught them the importance of being prepared for unexpected events and having a robust crisis management plan in place.

In summary, effective crisis management is essential for protecting a brand's reputation during times of trouble. Companies that develop comprehensive crisis management plans and communicate effectively during crises are better equipped to manage unexpected events and minimize the impact on their brand reputation and business operations.

14

The Importance of Emotional Connection in Branding

In today's competitive business landscape, creating a strong brand identity that resonates with customers is critical. One way to achieve this is by establishing an emotional connection with customers. Emotional connection refers to the feelings and associations customers have with a brand that go beyond functional benefits or features. Emotional connection creates a deeper bond between the customer and the brand, leading to increased loyalty, brand advocacy, and repeat purchases.

Brands that have successfully created an emotional connection with their customers have a significant advantage over their competitors. When customers feel an emotional connection to a brand, they are more likely to stay loyal to the brand, even if it means paying a higher price for its products or services. They are also more likely to recommend the brand to others and defend it against criticism.

One way to create emotional connections with customers is through storytelling. By sharing stories that align with the brand's values and mission, brands can create a narrative that resonates with customers. Storytelling allows brands to create an emotional connection by tapping into customers' emotions and creating a personal connection between the brand and the customer. For example, a brand that sells environmentally-friendly products can create an emotional connection with customers by sharing stories about the positive impact of its products on the environment.

Another way to create emotional connections is by establishing brand values that align with customers' values. Brands that demonstrate a commitment to social responsibility, environmental sustainability, and other causes that customers care about can create a strong emotional connection with customers. When customers see a brand taking a stand on issues they care about, they are more likely to feel a sense of loyalty and affinity towards that brand.

To create an emotional connection with customers, brands should also focus on creating a consistent and memorable customer experience. This includes everything from the visual identity of the brand to the way it interacts with customers on social media. A consistent and cohesive brand experience helps to create a sense of familiarity and trust between the brand and the customer, leading to a stronger emotional connection.

Explanation in the form of a story:
Once upon a time, there was a small coffee shop in the heart of a bustling city. The coffee shop had been around for years,

but it was struggling to compete with the big chain coffee shops that had recently opened up in the area.

The owner of the coffee shop, Maria, knew that she needed to do something to set her shop apart from the competition. She started by creating a new menu with unique drinks that couldn't be found anywhere else. But even with the new menu, Maria found that she was still struggling to attract customers.

One day, Maria had an idea. She decided to create a story that would help her customers connect with her brand on an emotional level. Maria grew up in a small town in South America, where she learned to make coffee from her grandmother. She decided to share this story with her customers.

Maria put up a large poster in her coffee shop that told the story of how she learned to make coffee from her grandmother. The poster had pictures of Maria's hometown and her grandmother's coffee farm. It also had a recipe for the special coffee blend that Maria learned to make from her grandmother.

Customers were immediately drawn to the story. They loved the personal connection that Maria had created with her brand. They also loved the unique coffee blend that Maria had created, which they couldn't find anywhere else.

Word quickly spread about Maria's coffee shop and its unique story. Customers started coming from all over the city to try Maria's special blend of coffee and hear her story. They even started bringing their friends and family to the coffee shop to share the experience.

Thanks to Maria's storytelling, her coffee shop became more than just a place to grab a cup of coffee. It became a place where customers could connect with a brand on an emotional level. Customers felt a personal connection to Maria and her coffee shop, which led to increased loyalty, brand advocacy, and repeat purchases.

In the end, Maria's coffee shop became one of the most popular coffee shops in the city. Her customers loved the unique experience that Maria had created, and they were willing to pay a higher price for her coffee because of the emotional connection they felt to her brand.

In conclusion, emotional connection plays a critical role in branding and building customer loyalty. Brands that can create an emotional connection with their customers are more likely to succeed in today's competitive business landscape. To create emotional connections with customers, brands should focus on storytelling, establish brand values that align with customers' values, and create a consistent and memorable customer experience.

15

Creating Brand Advocates: How to Turn Customers into Fans

In today's highly competitive marketplace, it's not enough to simply attract customers to your brand. The key to success lies in building a loyal customer base that will not only continue to support your brand but will also actively promote it to others. This is where brand advocates come in. Brand advocates are customers who are so passionate about your brand that they become vocal advocates for it. They share their positive experiences with others, post about your brand on social media, and even refer their friends and family to your business.

The importance of brand advocates cannot be overstated. According to a study by Nielsen, 92% of consumers trust recommendations from friends and family above all other forms of advertising. This means that having loyal customers who are willing to promote your brand can be a powerful marketing tool. Not only does it help you reach new customers, but it also builds trust and credibility for your brand.

So, how can you turn your customers into brand advocates? The key is to provide an exceptional customer experience. When your customers have a positive experience with your brand, they are more likely to become loyal customers and advocates for your brand.

Here are a few strategies to help you create brand advocates:

1. Provide Excellent Customer Service: The first step in creating brand advocates is to provide excellent customer service. This means going above and beyond to meet your customers' needs and expectations. When your customers feel valued and heard, they are more likely to become loyal customers and advocates for your brand.

2. Personalize Your Customer Experience: Customers want to feel like they are more than just a number. Personalizing your customer experience can go a long way in creating brand advocates. This can be as simple as addressing your customers by name or tailoring your marketing messages to their interests and preferences.

3. Incentivize Referrals: One of the most effective ways to turn customers into brand advocates is to incentivize referrals. Offer discounts, free products, or other incentives to customers who refer their friends and family to your business.

4. Create a Community: People want to feel like they are part of something. Creating a community around your brand can help foster a sense of belonging and loyalty among your customers. This can be done through social media, email newsletters, or even in-person events.

5. Share Your Brand Story: Your brand story is what sets you apart from your competitors. Sharing your brand story with your customers can help create an emotional connection and build trust. Make sure your brand story is authentic and aligns with your customers' values.

Explanation in the form of a story:

Once upon a time, there was a small business owner named Sarah who ran a local bakery. Sarah had a passion for baking and put her heart and soul into creating delicious treats for her customers. However, Sarah knew that simply providing great baked goods was not enough to compete with the larger chain bakeries in the area.

One day, Sarah had an idea. She realized that her loyal customers could be her greatest asset. She decided to focus on turning her customers into brand advocates who would actively promote her bakery to others.

Sarah began by providing excellent customer service. She greeted every customer with a smile and took the time to get to know them. She listened to their feedback and made adjustments to her products and services based on their needs and preferences.

Next, Sarah decided to personalize her customer experience. She started to address her regular customers by name and would often make personalized recommendations based on their past purchases. Her customers felt valued and appreciated, and they began to tell their friends and family about their positive experiences at Sarah's bakery.

Sarah also incentivized referrals by offering discounts to customers who referred new business to her bakery. This encouraged her loyal customers to spread the word about her bakery to their friends and family.

As Sarah's business grew, she decided to create a community around her brand. She started a Facebook group where she would share updates on her latest products and promotions. She also began to host in-person events, such as baking classes and tastings, where her customers could come together and connect with one another.

Finally, Sarah shared her brand story with her customers. She talked about how her passion for baking had led her to open her bakery and how she was committed to using only the finest ingredients in her products. Her customers appreciated her authenticity and began to feel a sense of pride in supporting a local business that shared their values.

Thanks to Sarah's efforts, her customers became more than just customers. They became loyal brand advocates who actively promoted her bakery to others. Her business grew, and she became a beloved fixture in the community.

In the end, Sarah realized that creating brand advocates was not just about increasing sales. It was about building meaningful relationships with her customers and creating a community of people who shared her passion for baking.

Quick examples:

1. Apple: Apple is a tech giant that has created a cult-like following among its customers. Apple's customers are so loyal that they will camp out in front of stores for days just to be the first to get their hands on the latest iPhone. Apple has achieved this level of loyalty by providing excellent customer service, creating a seamless user experience, and fostering a sense of community among its customers.

2. Nike: Nike is a brand that has successfully built a community of loyal customers through its marketing campaigns. Nike's "Just Do It" slogan has become synonymous with the brand and has inspired millions of people to push themselves to be their best. Nike also sponsors a number of high-profile athletes, which has helped to create an emotional connection between the brand and its customers.

3. Starbucks: Starbucks is a brand that has successfully personalized the customer experience. Starbucks' baristas are trained to remember their customers' names and drink orders, which helps to create a sense of familiarity and connection. Starbucks also offers a loyalty program that rewards customers for their purchases, which incentivizes repeat business and encourages customers to become brand advocates.

4. Glossier: Glossier is a beauty brand that has built a community of loyal customers through its social media presence. Glossier's Instagram feed is filled with user-generated content, which helps to create a sense of community among its customers. Glossier also encourages customers to share their experiences with the brand through its hashtag campaigns, which helps to spread the word about the brand to new customers.

In conclusion, brand advocates are an essential part of any successful marketing strategy. By providing excellent customer service, personalizing your customer experience, incentivizing referrals, creating a community, and sharing your brand story, you can turn your customers into loyal brand advocates who will help spread the word about your brand.

16

Leveraging User-Generated Content: Harnessing the Power of Your Community

User-generated content (UGC) refers to any content created by users, such as photos, videos, reviews, and social media posts, that promotes or relates to a brand or product. UGC has become increasingly popular as a marketing tool, as it can help brands build trust and credibility with their audience while increasing brand awareness and engagement.

One of the key advantages of UGC is that it's more authentic and relatable than branded content, which can often feel salesy or forced. UGC is created by real people who have a genuine interest in a brand or product, and this can help to establish a sense of community and trust around a brand.

UGC also has a higher likelihood of being shared, as people are more likely to engage with and share content created by their peers. This means that UGC can help to amplify a brand's reach and increase its visibility, especially on social media platforms where content can quickly go viral.

To encourage UGC, brands can take a number of different approaches. One effective strategy is to create a hashtag or campaign that encourages users to share their own content related to a brand or product. This could involve asking users to share photos or videos of themselves using the product, or to share their own tips and tricks for getting the most out of it.

Another popular approach is to run a UGC contest or giveaway. This can involve offering prizes or incentives for users who share the best content related to a brand or product. Contests can be run on social media platforms or on a brand's website, and can be a great way to generate buzz and engagement around a brand.

Brands can also leverage social media platforms to encourage UGC, by engaging with users who share content related to their brand and reposting or sharing that content on their own channels. This can help to establish a sense of community around a brand, and can encourage users to continue sharing content related to the brand.

It's important for brands to remember that UGC should be authentic and genuine, and not overly promotional or salesy. By encouraging users to share their own experiences and perspectives, brands can harness the power of their community to build trust, credibility, and engagement around their brand.

Explanation in the form of a story:

Once upon a time, there was a small fashion brand called "Bloom". The brand had been struggling to gain traction in a highly competitive market. They had tried various marketing strategies, but nothing seemed to work. Then, one day, the founder had an idea. "Why not ask our customers to help us promote our brand?" she thought.

The founder knew that their customers were passionate about their products and had a deep connection with the brand. She decided to launch a UGC campaign called "Bloom in your Style" on social media, where customers could share their pictures in Bloom's clothing using a specific hashtag.

The campaign quickly took off, with customers from all over the world sharing their pictures and personal stories about their experience with Bloom's clothing. The founder was thrilled to see the response and decided to take it a step further by organizing a contest where customers could win a chance to be featured on Bloom's website and social media pages.

As the campaign gained momentum, Bloom's community grew stronger, and customers felt a deeper connection to the brand. They were proud to be a part of the Bloom family and began to refer their friends and family to the brand.

The UGC campaign not only increased brand awareness but also helped Bloom to understand their customers better. They learned about their customer's preferences, style, and how they incorporated Bloom's clothing into their daily lives. This information helped the brand to improve its product offerings and tailor its marketing messages to better resonate with its target audience.

Thanks to the power of UGC, Bloom was able to establish itself as a unique and authentic brand that valued its community. The founder realized that by empowering her customers, she could harness the power of the community to drive growth and build brand loyalty. From that day on, Bloom continued to engage with its customers through UGC campaigns and create a thriving community of brand ambassadors who would support the brand through thick and thin.

Quick example:
Example 1: GoPro

GoPro is a popular action camera brand that has leveraged UGC to establish itself as the go-to brand for outdoor enthusiasts and adventure-seekers. GoPro's cameras are designed to capture action-packed footage, and the brand encourages its customers to share their footage on social media using the hashtag #GoPro.

GoPro's UGC strategy has been highly successful, with millions of people sharing their footage on social media platforms like Instagram, Facebook, and YouTube. GoPro regularly reposts user-generated content on its own social media channels, and the brand's official YouTube channel is filled with videos created by customers.

By leveraging UGC, GoPro has been able to establish itself as the leading brand for outdoor enthusiasts and adventure-seekers. Customers feel a deep connection to the brand and take pride in sharing their footage with the wider GoPro community. This sense of community has helped GoPro to build brand loyalty and drive sales.

Example 2: Glossier

Glossier is a beauty brand that has leveraged UGC to build a highly engaged and loyal customer base. The brand's UGC campaign, called "Skin First, Makeup Second," encourages customers to share pictures of their natural skin on social media using the hashtag #SkinFirst.

Glossier's UGC strategy has been highly successful, with thousands of customers sharing their pictures on Instagram and other social media platforms. Glossier regularly reposts user-generated content on its own social media channels and even features customer reviews on its website.

By leveraging UGC, Glossier has been able to establish itself as a brand that celebrates natural beauty and empowers women to feel confident in their own skin. Customers feel a deep connection to the brand and take pride in sharing their pictures with the wider Glossier community. This sense of community has helped Glossier to build brand loyalty and drive sales.

17

The Role of Influencers in Branding

In recent years, influencers have become an increasingly important part of modern branding strategies. Influencers are individuals who have built a loyal following on social media platforms such as Instagram, TikTok, and YouTube. These individuals have the power to sway the opinions and purchasing decisions of their followers, making them a valuable asset for businesses looking to build brand awareness and trust.

The Role of Influencers in Modern Branding

The role of influencers in modern branding is multifaceted. Here are some key ways in which influencers can help build brand awareness and trust:

Reach a wider audience: Influencers have a large and engaged following on social media platforms. Partnering with influencers can help brands reach a wider audience than they would be able to on their own.

Establish credibility: Influencers are seen as experts or authorities in their niche. By partnering with an influencer, a brand can leverage their credibility and establish themselves as a trusted source in that niche.

Build trust: Influencers have built a relationship with their followers based on trust. By partnering with an influencer, a brand can tap into that trust and build a relationship with the influencer's followers.

Create engaging content: Influencers are skilled at creating engaging content that resonates with their audience. By partnering with an influencer, a brand can create content that is more likely to be shared and engaged with.

Identifying and Working with Influencers

Identifying and working with influencers can be a complex process. Here are some steps you can take to identify and work with influencers:

Identify the right influencers: The first step is to identify influencers who align with your brand values and target audience. Look for influencers who are active in your niche and have a large and engaged following.

Build a relationship: Once you have identified influencers who are a good fit for your brand, start building a relationship with them. Follow them on social media, engage with their content, and share their posts.

Negotiate partnerships: When negotiating partnerships with influencers, be clear about your expectations and goals. Be prepared to offer influencers compensation, such as free products or payment, in exchange for their promotion of your brand.

Measure ROI: It's important to track the success of your influencer campaigns. Monitor metrics such as engagement, website traffic, and sales to determine the ROI of your partnerships with influencers.

Explanation in the form of a story:

Once upon a time, there was a small skincare company that had recently launched a new line of natural, organic products. The company had a loyal customer base but was struggling to reach a wider audience and establish themselves as a trusted source in the crowded skincare market.

One day, the company's marketing team had an idea - they decided to partner with a popular beauty influencer on Instagram. They identified an influencer who aligned with their brand values and had a large and engaged following.

The marketing team started building a relationship with the influencer by following her on social media, engaging with her content, and sharing her posts. They also reached out to her and explained their brand values, the benefits of their products, and their goals for the partnership.

After some negotiations, the influencer agreed to promote the company's products on her Instagram feed and in her stories. She created a series of posts featuring the products, explaining their benefits and sharing her own experience using them. She also included a discount code for her followers to use when purchasing the products.

The influencer's posts generated a lot of engagement and interest in the company's products. The company saw a significant increase in website traffic and sales, and they were able to reach a wider audience and establish themselves as a trusted source in the skincare market.

As a result of the successful partnership, the company continued to work with the influencer on future campaigns and saw continued growth and success. They also started working with other influencers who aligned with their brand values and target audience, further expanding their reach and building trust with their customers.

In conclusion, this story illustrates how influencers can play a powerful role in modern branding by helping businesses to reach a wider audience, establish credibility, and build trust with their customers. By identifying and working with influencers who align with their brand values and target audience, businesses can leverage the power of social media to grow and succeed in today's competitive market.

In conclusion, influencers play an important role in modern branding by helping to build brand awareness and trust. To identify and work with influencers, businesses should focus on building relationships with influencers who align with their brand values and target audience, negotiate partnerships, and measure the ROI of their influencer campaigns.

18

Crafting Memorable Brand Experiences: Events, Pop-Ups, and Experiential Marketing

Creating memorable brand experiences is essential in building brand loyalty and engaging with consumers. Consumers don't just buy products, they buy experiences, and crafting a memorable brand experience is an effective way to connect with them. A memorable brand experience can be created through events, pop-ups, and experiential marketing. In this response, we will discuss the importance of creating memorable brand experiences, how they can help build brand loyalty, and offer guidance on how to plan and execute successful brand experiences.

Why Creating Memorable Brand Experiences is Important

Creating a memorable brand experience is important for several reasons:

1. Creates Emotional Connection: When consumers have an emotional connection to a brand, they are more likely to be loyal to it. By creating a memorable brand experience, brands can create emotional connections with their consumers and foster loyalty.
2. Differentiation: In today's competitive market, it's essential for brands to differentiate themselves from their competitors. A memorable brand experience can help a brand stand out from the crowd and differentiate itself from its competitors.
3. Word of Mouth: When consumers have a positive experience with a brand, they are more likely to tell others about it. Creating a memorable brand experience can encourage word-of-mouth marketing and generate buzz around the brand.
4. Consumer Engagement: A memorable brand experience can engage consumers and make them feel like they are part of the brand's story. This engagement can lead to increased brand awareness, positive sentiment, and ultimately, increased sales.

How Memorable Brand Experiences Can Help Build Brand Loyalty

Memorable brand experiences can help build brand loyalty in several ways:

1. Emotional Connection: When consumers have an emotional connection to a brand, they are more likely to be loyal to it. By creating a memorable brand experience, brands can create emotional connections with their consumers and foster loyalty.

2. Positive Sentiment: A memorable brand experience can create positive sentiment towards a brand. Consumers who have a positive experience with a brand are more likely to become loyal customers.

3. Word-of-Mouth: When consumers have a positive experience with a brand, they are more likely to tell others about it. This word-of-mouth marketing can lead to increased brand awareness and increased sales.

4. Personalization: A memorable brand experience can be personalized to each consumer, making them feel valued and appreciated. This personalization can lead to increased loyalty and brand advocacy.

How to Plan and Execute Successful Brand Experiences

Planning and executing successful brand experiences can be challenging, but here are some tips to help:

1. Define Your Objectives: Before planning your brand experience, define your objectives. What do you want to achieve with this experience? Do you want to increase brand awareness or generate buzz around a new product? Once you define your objectives, you can plan your experience accordingly.

2. Know Your Target Audience: Understanding your target audience is essential in creating a successful brand experience. What are their interests and preferences? What do they expect from your brand? Knowing your target audience can help you create a personalized and memorable experience.

3. Create a Memorable Experience: To create a memorable brand experience, you need to think outside the box. What

can you do to engage your audience and create a lasting impression? Consider incorporating interactive elements, such as virtual reality, or offering unique experiences, such as exclusive access to a product or service.

4. Choose the Right Venue: Choosing the right venue is essential in creating a successful brand experience. Consider the location, size, and accessibility of the venue. Will it accommodate your target audience? Will it enhance your brand experience?

5. Promote Your Event: Promoting your event is essential in generating buzz and attracting your target audience. Use social media, email marketing, and influencers to promote your event and reach a wider audience.

Explanation in the form of a story:

Once upon a time, there was a small coffee shop called "Café Bliss" that was struggling to attract new customers. The owner, Maria, knew she needed to do something to stand out from her competitors and create a memorable brand experience.

Maria decided to host a pop-up event in a nearby park on a sunny Saturday morning. She spent weeks planning the event and creating a unique experience for her customers.

On the day of the event, Maria and her team set up a cozy and inviting atmosphere with blankets, pillows, and books for customers to relax and enjoy their coffee. They also created a photo booth with props and a Café Bliss logo backdrop, encouraging customers to take pictures and share them on social media.

But what really made the event memorable was the interactive coffee-making station. Maria had hired a professional barista to teach customers how to make latte art, and they could practice making designs on their own cups. It was a hit, and customers were taking pictures and videos of their creations and sharing them on social media with the hashtag #CaféBlissPopUp.

Maria also offered a limited edition "Café Bliss Pop-Up Blend" of coffee for customers to take home and enjoy. And as a surprise, she gave away free "Café Bliss" t-shirts to the first ten customers who arrived at the event.

The pop-up event was a huge success, and customers couldn't stop talking about their experience at Café Bliss. They shared their pictures and videos on social media, wrote positive reviews online, and told their friends about the unique and memorable experience they had at the pop-up.

As a result, Café Bliss attracted a new group of loyal customers who appreciated the personalization, unique experience, and attention to detail that Maria had put into the pop-up event. The café's sales increased, and the buzz generated from the pop-up event continued to drive business even after it was over.

In this story, Café Bliss created a memorable brand experience through a pop-up event that engaged customers, offered personalized experiences, and encouraged social sharing. By planning and executing a successful brand experience, Café Bliss was able to stand out from competitors, build brand loyalty, and increase sales.

19

Personal Branding: How to Build Your Own Professional Image

Personal branding is the process of creating and maintaining a professional image and reputation for yourself. It involves promoting your skills, experiences, and values to build a positive impression among your colleagues, clients, and potential employers. Building a strong personal brand can help you stand out in a competitive job market, establish yourself as an expert in your field, and open up new career opportunities.

Importance of Personal Branding

Personal branding is essential in today's professional world as it can help you create a positive and lasting impression on your audience. A strong personal brand can help you achieve the following:

Build Credibility and Trust: A strong personal brand can help you establish yourself as an authority in your field. By consistently sharing valuable content and showcasing your expertise, you can build credibility and trust among your audience.

Differentiate Yourself: In a crowded job market, having a unique personal brand can help you stand out. By highlighting your unique skills, experiences, and values, you can differentiate yourself from others in your field.

Enhance Your Professional Network: Personal branding can help you expand your professional network by connecting with other professionals who share your interests and values.

Boost Your Career: A strong personal brand can help you attract new job opportunities and advance your career. By showcasing your skills and experiences, you can position yourself as a valuable asset to potential employers.

Developing and Maintaining a Strong Personal Brand

Here are some tips to help you build and maintain a strong personal brand:

Define Your Personal Brand: The first step in building your personal brand is to define your goals, values, and unique strengths. Identify your target audience and tailor your messaging to resonate with them.

Build Your Online Presence: Your online presence is a critical aspect of your personal brand. Create a professional website or blog and regularly update it with relevant content. Use social media to share your expertise and connect with others in your field.

Network with Others: Attend industry events and conferences, and connect with other professionals in your field. Participate in online communities and forums to share your insights and connect with like-minded individuals.

Be Consistent: Consistency is key when it comes to personal branding. Ensure that your messaging and visual branding are consistent across all your online and offline channels.

Monitor Your Online Reputation: Monitor your online reputation regularly and respond promptly to any negative feedback or comments.

Explanation in the form of a story:

Krishna Mohan Avancha is a digital marketing expert with over 20 years of experience in the field of search engine optimization (SEO), lead generation, and online marketing. He has worked with various top-tier organizations and startups in the US, Europe, and India, establishing himself as a thought leader in the industry.

Krishna's personal branding journey started by defining his unique strengths and experiences. He focused on developing his expertise in digital marketing and SEO, and became known as an expert in these areas. He created a professional website and social media profiles, where he regularly shares his insights and thoughts on the latest trends in digital marketing.

Krishna's consistent efforts to build his personal brand have helped him establish a strong reputation in the industry. He has been invited to speak at various conferences and has been featured in several publications. Krishna's personal brand has helped him attract new career opportunities and establish himself as a thought leader in his field.

Krishna has several salient advantages over others in the same genre due to his strong personal brand. Some of these advantages include:

Credibility and Trust: Krishna's consistent efforts to share his insights and thoughts on the latest trends in digital marketing and SEO have helped him establish credibility and trust among his audience.

Differentiation: Krishna's unique strengths and expertise in digital marketing and SEO have helped him differentiate himself from others in his field.

Professional Network: Krishna's strong personal brand has helped him expand his professional network and connect with other professionals in his field.

Career Opportunities: Krishna's personal brand has helped him attract new job opportunities and establish himself as a valuable asset to potential employers.

In conclusion, Krishna Mohan Avancha's personal branding journey serves as an excellent example of how building a strong personal brand can help establish oneself as an expert in their field. His consistent efforts to share his insights and thoughts on digital marketing and SEO have helped him differentiate himself from others and attract new career opportunities.

You can build your own personal brand by following the below steps:

1. Define Your Personal Brand: Start by defining your unique strengths, values, and goals. Identify your target audience and tailor your messaging to resonate with them. Be authentic and consistent in your communication to build a strong personal brand.

2. Build Your Online Presence: Your online presence is critical to building a professional image. Create a professional website or blog, and regularly update it with relevant content. Use social media to share your expertise and connect with others in your field. Keep your online profiles up to date and professional.

3. Network with Others: Attend industry events and conferences, and connect with other professionals in your field. Participate in online communities and forums to share your insights and connect with like-minded individuals. Join professional organizations and take advantage of networking opportunities.

4. Be Proactive: Take charge of your professional development by staying informed about the latest trends and technologies in your field. Continuously improve your skills and knowledge through training, workshops, and online courses.

5. Showcase Your Achievements: Share your achievements and successes with your network. Highlight your skills,

experiences, and accomplishments to build your credibility and reputation. Be humble but confident in your abilities.

By following these examples, you can build a strong professional image that will help you stand out in your field and achieve your career goals. Remember, building a professional image takes time and effort, but the rewards are worth it. With consistent effort and dedication, you can establish yourself as an expert in your field and build a successful career.

In summary, personal branding is a powerful tool for building a professional image and reputation. By defining your personal brand, building your online presence, networking with others, and being consistent, you can develop and maintain a strong personal brand that can help you achieve your career goals.

20

Building a Brand for a Non-Profit or Social Enterprise

Building a brand for a non-profit or social enterprise requires a unique approach compared to building a brand for a for-profit business. While the ultimate goal may still be to establish a strong reputation, attract supporters, and achieve organizational objectives, the context and priorities of non-profits and social enterprises are different. In this article, we will explore the unique considerations for branding non-profits and social enterprises and offer guidance on how to build a strong brand.

Unique Considerations for Branding Non-Profits and Social Enterprises:

Mission-driven: Non-profits and social enterprises are mission-driven organizations. They exist to address a specific social or environmental issue, and their brand should reflect that mission. The brand should convey the organization's purpose and values, and it should resonate with the target audience.

Stakeholder-focused: Non-profits and social enterprises have multiple stakeholders, including donors, volunteers, beneficiaries, and partners. Each stakeholder group has different needs and expectations, and the brand should appeal to all of them. The brand should also reflect the organization's commitment to transparency, accountability, and impact.

Limited resources: Non-profits and social enterprises often have limited financial and human resources, which can make it challenging to invest in branding. However, branding is essential for attracting support and achieving the organization's goals. Therefore, non-profits and social enterprises should prioritize branding efforts that are cost-effective and efficient.

Storytelling: Non-profits and social enterprises have compelling stories to tell. Their work often involves overcoming significant challenges, helping vulnerable populations, and making a positive impact on society. The brand should reflect these stories and use them to engage and inspire supporters.

Guidance on Building a Strong Brand for Non-Profits and Social Enterprises:

Develop a clear brand strategy: Before developing any branding materials, it is essential to develop a clear brand strategy. This strategy should include the organization's mission, values, target audience, messaging, and visual identity. The brand strategy should guide all branding efforts and ensure consistency across all channels.

Tell compelling stories: Non-profits and social enterprises should use storytelling to communicate their impact and engage supporters. Stories should be authentic, emotional, and demonstrate the organization's mission and values. These stories can be told through various channels, such as social media, videos, and annual reports.

Leverage partnerships: Non-profits and social enterprises can leverage partnerships to build their brand and extend their reach. Partnerships can include collaborations with other non-profits, businesses, or influencers. Partnerships can help non-profits and social enterprises reach new audiences and build credibility.

Invest in a strong visual identity: Non-profits and social enterprises should invest in a strong visual identity, including a logo, color scheme, and visual elements. The visual identity should be consistent across all channels and help communicate the organization's mission and values.

Engage supporters: Non-profits and social enterprises should engage their supporters through various channels, such as social media, email, and events. Engaging supporters can help build a community around the organization's mission and increase support.

Explanation in the form of a story:
Meet Maria, the founder of a social enterprise that aims to reduce plastic waste in her community. Maria's social enterprise, called "Green Waves," collects and recycles plastic waste and produces eco-friendly products.

When Maria started her social enterprise, she knew that branding would be critical to attracting support and achieving her mission. However, Maria also recognized that building a brand for a social enterprise would require a unique approach.

Maria developed a clear brand strategy that reflected her organization's mission and values. She wanted Green Waves' brand to convey the importance of reducing plastic waste and promoting sustainability. She also identified her target audience, which included eco-conscious consumers, schools, and local businesses.

To tell compelling stories, Maria shared the personal stories of the people who benefited from Green Waves' work. She interviewed local residents who were impacted by plastic waste and shared how Green Waves' products helped them reduce their environmental footprint. Maria also shared behind-the-scenes stories of the challenges and successes of building a social enterprise.

To leverage partnerships, Maria collaborated with local businesses and schools to promote Green Waves' mission. She partnered with a local coffee shop that used Green Waves' eco-friendly cups and offered discounts to customers who brought in their own reusable cups. Maria also partnered with schools to host educational workshops on reducing plastic waste.

To invest in a strong visual identity, Maria worked with a local designer to create a logo, color scheme, and visual elements that reflected Green Waves' mission and values. She ensured that the visual identity was consistent across all channels, including social media, website, and packaging.

Finally, to engage supporters, Maria used various channels, such as social media, email, and events. She created a Facebook page where she shared Green Waves' work and engaged with supporters. She also hosted community events, such as beach cleanups and sustainability fairs, where supporters could learn more about Green Waves' work.

Thanks to Maria's branding efforts, Green Waves' brand has become synonymous with sustainability and reducing plastic waste in the community. People recognize Green Waves' products and support their mission. Green Waves has gained a loyal following of supporters and has been able to expand its operations and impact.

In conclusion, Maria's story shows how a social enterprise can build a strong brand by developing a clear brand strategy, telling compelling stories, leveraging partnerships, investing in a strong visual identity, and engaging supporters. These branding strategies help social enterprises establish a strong reputation, attract support, and achieve their mission.

In conclusion, building a brand for a non-profit or social enterprise requires a unique approach. Non-profits and social enterprises are mission-driven, stakeholder-focused, have limited resources, and have compelling stories to tell. To build a strong brand, non-profits and social enterprises should develop a clear brand strategy, tell compelling stories, leverage partnerships, invest in a strong visual identity, and engage supporters. With these strategies, non-profits and social enterprises can establish a strong brand that resonates with their target audience and helps them achieve their mission.

21

Scaling Your Brand: Growing Beyond Your Initial Audience

Scaling a brand is a challenging process, but it also presents significant opportunities for growth and expansion. When a brand begins to grow beyond its initial audience, it can attract new customers, increase revenue, and gain a stronger foothold in the market. However, this growth also brings new challenges and requires careful planning and execution.

One of the main challenges of scaling a brand is maintaining the core values and identity that made it successful in the first place. As a brand grows, it may need to adapt to new markets and customer segments, but it's important not to lose sight of what made the brand unique and appealing to its initial audience. It's also essential to maintain consistency in branding and messaging across all channels and touchpoints, to ensure that the brand remains recognizable and trustworthy to new audiences.

Another challenge of scaling a brand is managing resources

effectively. As a brand grows, it may need to expand its team, invest in new technology, and allocate more resources to marketing and advertising. However, it's crucial to balance these investments with financial sustainability and ensure that the brand is generating enough revenue to support its growth.

Despite these challenges, scaling a brand can be highly rewarding. Here are some strategies to consider when expanding your brand's reach:

Partner with complementary brands: Collaborating with other brands that share your target audience can be an effective way to expand your reach and tap into new markets. Look for brands that have a similar brand identity and values, but offer complementary products or services.

Invest in targeted marketing campaigns: As your brand expands, it's important to reach new audiences through targeted marketing campaigns. Identify the channels and platforms that are most effective in reaching your target audience, and invest in advertising and content that speaks directly to their needs and interests.

Create valuable content: Content marketing is an effective way to build brand awareness and engage with new audiences. Focus on creating content that provides value to your target audience, whether it's informative blog posts, how-to guides, or entertaining social media content.

Leverage social media: Social media can be a powerful tool for reaching new audiences and building brand awareness. Focus on building a strong social media presence by engaging with your followers, sharing valuable content, and collaborating with influencers and other brands.

Expand into new markets: Consider expanding your brand into new geographic or demographic markets. Conduct research to understand the needs and preferences of these new audiences, and adapt your branding and messaging accordingly.

In summary, scaling a brand can be a challenging but rewarding process. To expand your brand's reach, it's essential to maintain consistency in branding and messaging, manage resources effectively, and invest in targeted marketing campaigns, valuable content, and strategic partnerships. By following these strategies, your brand can continue to grow and thrive beyond its initial audience.

Explanation in the form of a story:

Imagine a small local bakery that has gained a loyal following in their neighborhood. They're known for their delicious, freshly baked bread and pastries, and their customers love the warm, welcoming atmosphere of the shop. However, the bakery owner, Sarah, is starting to think about expanding her business beyond the local community.

Sarah knows that expanding her brand will be a significant challenge. She's proud of the unique identity and values that have made her bakery successful, and she doesn't want to compromise those in pursuit of growth. She's also aware that she'll need to invest in new resources, including marketing and advertising, to reach new audiences.

To begin the expansion process, Sarah decides to partner with a local coffee shop. The coffee shop has a similar target audience and shares Sarah's commitment to quality and community. Together, they create a joint marketing campaign, offering a discount on coffee and pastries when customers visit both shops.

The campaign is a huge success, attracting new customers to both businesses and creating a buzz in the community. Encouraged by the response, Sarah decides to invest in a social media campaign, featuring mouth-watering photos of her bread and pastries and engaging with customers online.

As the bakery's reputation grows, Sarah realizes that she needs to expand her team to keep up with demand. She hires new staff and invests in new technology to streamline operations and improve efficiency. She's careful to maintain the same level of quality and attention to detail that has made her bakery successful, even as the business grows.

Finally, Sarah decides to expand into a new market by offering delivery services to neighboring towns. She conducts extensive research to understand the needs and preferences of these new customers and adapts her branding and messaging accordingly. She also hires a marketing agency to create targeted campaigns that speak directly to these new audiences.

Through a combination of strategic partnerships, targeted marketing campaigns, and careful resource management, Sarah is able to successfully scale her bakery beyond its initial audience. The bakery continues to thrive, attracting new customers while maintaining its unique identity and commitment to quality and community.

Quick example:

Let's say you're the owner of a small, eco-friendly clothing brand that sells sustainable and ethically-made clothing. You've been successful in attracting a niche audience of environmentally conscious consumers, but you're looking to expand your brand's reach and tap into new markets. Here are some strategies you could consider:

Partner with complementary brands: You could partner with a vegan shoe company that shares your target audience and values. You could collaborate on a joint marketing campaign or offer a bundled discount for customers who purchase from both brands.

Invest in targeted marketing campaigns: You could invest in targeted social media advertising to reach new audiences who are interested in sustainable fashion. You could also run targeted email campaigns to previous customers who haven't made a purchase in a while, offering them a special discount to encourage repeat business.

Create valuable content: You could create informative blog posts or videos that highlight the benefits of sustainable clothing or offer tips on how to shop ethically. You could also use social media to share behind-the-scenes content or showcase the people and processes behind your brand.

109

Leverage social media: You could collaborate with influencers or micro-influencers who share your brand's values and target audience. You could also use social media to engage with your followers and showcase user-generated content featuring your brand.

Expand into new markets: You could expand your brand into new geographic markets, such as Europe or Asia, where there is growing demand for sustainable fashion. You could also consider expanding into new demographics, such as the men's or children's clothing markets.

By following these strategies, you can expand your brand's reach and tap into new markets, while still maintaining your core values and identity.

22

The Role of Partnerships in Branding

Partnerships have become an integral part of modern branding, as they offer an effective way to build brand awareness and reach new audiences. A partnership is a strategic alliance between two or more companies or organizations with complementary products, services, or values that work together to achieve mutually beneficial goals.

The importance of partnerships in branding lies in their ability to leverage the strengths of each partner and create value for the end consumer. By collaborating with another brand, companies can tap into new markets, gain access to new audiences, and increase their brand recognition. Additionally, partnerships can be an excellent way to differentiate a brand from its competitors and strengthen its position in the marketplace.

Here are some of the ways partnerships can help build brand awareness and reach new audiences:

Increased exposure: Partnering with another brand can help increase exposure and reach for both companies. By leveraging each other's audiences, brands can attract new customers and build brand awareness.

Enhanced credibility: Partnerships can also enhance the credibility and reputation of a brand. When a brand associates itself with another reputable brand, it can improve its image and reputation.

Increased innovation: Partnerships can be a catalyst for innovation. By collaborating with other brands, companies can bring new products and services to market faster and more efficiently.

To identify and build successful partnerships, companies should consider the following factors:

Alignment of values: Brands should look for partners that share their values and mission. A partnership built on shared values is more likely to be successful and long-lasting.

Complementary products or services: Partnerships should be built between companies with complementary products or services. This ensures that the partnership is mutually beneficial and provides value to the end consumer.

Reach and audience: Brands should also consider the reach and audience of potential partners. A partnership with a brand that has a large and engaged audience can help increase exposure and reach for both companies.

Negotiating and measuring ROI: When building partnerships, it is essential to negotiate clear objectives and goals for the partnership. Companies should also establish clear metrics for measuring the success of the partnership, such as ROI, engagement, or increased sales. This will help ensure that the partnership is successful and delivers value for both partners.

Quick example:
One example is the partnership between GoPro and Red Bull. GoPro is a company that produces action cameras, while Red Bull is an energy drink brand that is known for sponsoring extreme sports events. Both brands share a common target audience: young, active, and adventurous individuals who enjoy extreme sports.

The partnership between GoPro and Red Bull involves co-sponsoring various events and competitions, such as the Red Bull X-Fighters, Red Bull Cliff Diving, and the Red Bull Air Race. GoPro provides cameras to capture footage of the events, while Red Bull uses the footage in its marketing campaigns and social media channels to showcase the thrilling experiences of its sponsored athletes.

This partnership has been successful for both brands, as it has helped them reach new audiences and increase brand awareness. By collaborating, GoPro and Red Bull have been able to leverage each other's strengths to create engaging content and connect with their shared target audience.

Furthermore, this partnership has allowed both brands to differentiate themselves from their competitors. GoPro is no longer just a camera company, but also a brand associated with extreme sports and adventure. Similarly, Red Bull is not just an energy drink, but a brand that supports and sponsors extreme sports and athletes.

To measure the success of their partnership, GoPro and Red Bull have established clear metrics, such as the number of social media impressions, video views, and engagement rates. By tracking these metrics, they can evaluate the ROI of their partnership and make adjustments to their strategy if necessary.

In conclusion, the partnership between GoPro and Red Bull is an excellent example of how partnerships can help build brand awareness, reach new audiences, and differentiate a brand from its competitors. By finding a partner with complementary values, products, and audiences, brands can create a mutually beneficial alliance that delivers value for both partners and their customers.

Explanation in the form of a story:

Once upon a time, there was a small clothing brand called "Sunflower Apparel" that wanted to increase its brand awareness and reach a wider audience. They had a unique style that was perfect for music festival-goers and wanted to connect with that audience. However, they didn't have the budget to run a large-scale marketing campaign to reach this demographic.

One day, they had an idea. They reached out to a local music festival that aligned with their values and style and proposed a partnership. The music festival was excited about the opportunity to work with a local brand and agreed to the partnership.

Together, Sunflower Apparel and the music festival created a co-branded clothing line that was sold exclusively at the festival. The clothing line featured Sunflower Apparel's unique style with the festival's branding and theme. The clothing was a hit with festival-goers, who loved the unique style and exclusivity of the co-branded line.

In addition to the clothing line, Sunflower Apparel and the festival created a social media campaign that showcased the clothing and promoted the festival. The campaign included influencer partnerships, social media giveaways, and behind-the-scenes content that gave followers a sneak peek into the partnership.

The partnership was a huge success for both Sunflower Apparel and the music festival. Sunflower Apparel was able to reach a wider audience and connect with their target demographic in a meaningful way. The festival was able to offer a unique and exclusive clothing line that resonated with their audience and helped increase ticket sales.

By working together, Sunflower Apparel and the music festival were able to create a partnership that delivered value for both partners and their customers. They were able to leverage each other's strengths to create something unique and memorable. The success of the partnership inspired Sunflower Apparel to pursue similar collaborations with other festivals and events, leading to continued growth and success for the brand.

In conclusion, partnerships have become an important tool in modern branding. By building strategic alliances with other brands, companies can reach new audiences, increase brand awareness, and differentiate themselves from their competitors. To identify and build successful partnerships, brands should focus on finding partners with shared values and complementary products or services, negotiate clear objectives and goals, and establish metrics for measuring ROI.

23

Branding on a Budget: How to Create a Strong Identity with Limited Resources

Branding on a budget can be a challenging task, especially for small businesses and startups with limited resources. Creating a strong brand identity requires time, effort, and money, and it can be tough to figure out where to start. However, with the right strategies and tools, it is possible to build a strong brand without breaking the bank. Here are some tips on how to create a strong brand identity with limited resources:

Define your brand

The first step in creating a strong brand identity is to define your brand. This includes understanding your brand's purpose, values, personality, and target audience. Conduct market research to gather insights about your target audience's preferences, needs, and behavior. This will help you create a brand that resonates with your audience and stands out from

117

your competitors.

Develop your brand assets

Once you have defined your brand, you need to develop your brand assets. These include your logo, color palette, typography, and imagery. You don't necessarily need to hire a professional designer to create your brand assets. You can use online tools like Canva, which offers a range of templates and design elements to create professional-looking designs for free or at a low cost.

Create a consistent brand voice

Your brand voice is the tone and style of your communication with your audience. It includes the language, messaging, and style of your content. Creating a consistent brand voice is essential for building brand recognition and loyalty. You can achieve this by developing a style guide that outlines your brand voice and tone. This will ensure that all your communications, whether it's social media posts, blog articles, or email newsletters, have a consistent voice and messaging.

Leverage social media

Social media is a powerful tool for building brand awareness and engagement. It is also a cost-effective way to promote your brand and reach your target audience. Choose the social media platforms that your target audience uses and create a content strategy that aligns with your brand voice and values. You can use online tools like Hootsuite, Buffer, or Later to schedule your social media posts in advance and save time.

Collaborate with influencers

Influencer marketing is a popular marketing strategy that involves partnering with social media influencers to promote your brand. It can be an effective way to reach a new audience and build brand credibility. You don't necessarily need to collaborate with big-name influencers with a large following. Micro-influencers, with a smaller but engaged following, can be just as effective and more affordable.

Measure and adjust

Finally, it's important to measure your branding efforts' effectiveness and adjust your strategy accordingly. Use online tools like Google Analytics or social media analytics to track your brand's reach, engagement, and conversion rates. This will help you identify what works and what doesn't and adjust your branding strategy accordingly.

Quick example:

Let's say you're starting a small organic coffee shop in a trendy neighborhood. You want to create a brand that resonates with health-conscious and environmentally conscious coffee drinkers. Here's how you can build a strong brand identity on a budget:

Define your brand

You conduct market research and find that your target audience is interested in organic, fair-trade coffee, and sustainability. You define your brand as an ethical and eco-friendly coffee shop that offers premium quality coffee to health-conscious consumers.

Develop your brand assets

119

You use Canva to create a simple yet memorable logo that incorporates green and brown colors to symbolize sustainability and organic farming. You choose a modern yet easy-to-read font for your brand name and tagline. You create a simple website that showcases your brand story, menu, and location.

Create a consistent brand voice

You develop a style guide that outlines your brand voice and tone. You choose a friendly yet informative tone for your communication with customers. You use social media to engage with your customers and share your brand values and mission. You create a blog that features articles about the health benefits of coffee, sustainability, and fair trade.

Leverage social media

You use Instagram and Facebook to share high-quality photos of your coffee, your shop, and your customers enjoying your coffee. You use relevant hashtags and location tags to reach local coffee lovers. You respond promptly to customer inquiries and feedback and use social media analytics to track your engagement and reach.

Collaborate with influencers

You identify local micro-influencers who share your brand values and offer them free coffee in exchange for sharing their experience with their followers. You also offer a discount to customers who bring their reusable cups and encourage them to post photos on social media and tag your shop.

Measure and adjust

You use Google Analytics to track your website traffic and

conversion rates. You notice that your blog articles about sustainability and fair trade get more engagement and shares than your menu items. You adjust your content strategy to focus more on educating your customers about your brand values and mission.

By following these steps, you can create a strong brand identity for your coffee shop without spending a lot of money on branding agencies or advertising. You can build a loyal customer base that shares your brand values and supports your mission.

Explanation in the form of a story:

Once upon a time, there was a small business owner named Sarah. She had a great idea for a product, but she didn't have a lot of money to invest in branding and marketing. Sarah knew that building a strong brand identity was essential for her business's success, but she wasn't sure where to start.

Sarah began by researching her target audience and understanding their preferences and needs. She discovered that her target audience valued sustainability and ethical practices, which aligned with her product's values. She used this insight to define her brand's purpose and personality.

Next, Sarah needed to develop her brand assets, including her logo, color palette, and imagery. She couldn't afford to hire a professional designer, so she decided to use online design tools like Canva to create her brand assets. She spent time experimenting with different designs until she found something that reflected her brand's values and personality.

Sarah also created a consistent brand voice by developing a style guide that outlined her brand's tone and messaging. She made sure that all her communications, from her website to her social media posts, had a consistent voice and messaging.

To promote her brand, Sarah leveraged social media and collaborated with influencers who shared her values. She used online tools like Hootsuite to schedule her social media posts in advance and save time. She also reached out to micro-influencers who had a smaller but engaged following and offered them free products in exchange for promoting her brand.

Finally, Sarah measured her branding efforts' effectiveness and adjusted her strategy accordingly. She used Google Analytics and social media analytics to track her brand's reach, engagement, and conversion rates. She learned what worked and what didn't and made changes to her branding strategy accordingly.

Over time, Sarah's branding efforts paid off. Her brand gained a loyal following of customers who shared her values and appreciated her product's quality. Her business grew, and she was able to invest more money in branding and marketing. Sarah realized that building a strong brand identity on a limited budget was challenging, but it was possible with creativity, strategy, and persistence.

In conclusion, building a strong brand identity on a limited budget requires a combination of creativity, strategy, and persistence. By defining your brand, developing your brand assets, creating a consistent brand voice, leveraging social media, collaborating with influencers, and measuring your results, you can create a brand that resonates with your target audience and stands out from your competitors.

24

Legal Considerations in Branding: Trademarks, Copyrights, and Intellectual Property

Legal considerations in branding are important to ensure that your brand is protected from infringement and misuse by others. Three main areas of legal consideration in branding are trademarks, copyrights, and intellectual property.

Trademarks are distinctive symbols, logos, or phrases that identify and distinguish a company's products or services from those of other companies. They can be registered with the United States Patent and Trademark Office (USPTO) to obtain legal protection. Registering a trademark can help prevent others from using a similar symbol or name that may confuse consumers or dilute the value of your brand. It's essential to choose a unique and memorable name or logo to avoid any confusion with existing trademarks.

Copyrights are a type of intellectual property protection that grants the creator of an original work the exclusive right to reproduce, distribute, and display their work. Copyright protection applies to a wide range of creative works, including logos, slogans, advertising copy, and other branding materials. Registering a copyright with the United States Copyright Office can provide additional legal protection.

Intellectual property (IP) refers to a wide range of intangible assets, including trademarks, copyrights, patents, and trade secrets. IP protection is essential to safeguard the unique features of a brand or product, such as its logo, name, design, or innovation. Companies can protect their IP rights by registering their trademarks, copyrights, and patents and enforcing these rights through legal action against infringers.

To protect your brand legally, it's essential to take proactive steps, such as:

Conducting a trademark search to ensure that your brand name and logo are unique and not already registered by another company.

Registering your trademarks with the USPTO and renewing them periodically to maintain legal protection.

Creating and implementing a comprehensive brand style guide that outlines the proper use of your brand assets, including logos, colors, and typography.

Obtaining permission or licenses for the use of third-party copyrighted materials.

Monitoring your brand and taking legal action against in-fringers who misuse your brand or intellectual property.

Quick example:

Let's say you have a startup company that produces organic food products and you want to create a brand name and logo for your company. Before finalizing your brand identity, it's important to conduct a thorough trademark search to ensure that the name and logo you're considering are not already in use by another company. You can use resources such as the USPTO's trademark database or hire a trademark attorney to conduct a comprehensive search.

Assuming you've completed your trademark search and found that your brand name and logo are available, you can proceed to register your trademarks with the USPTO to obtain legal protection. By registering your trademarks, you can prevent other companies from using a similar name or logo that may confuse consumers and dilute the value of your brand.

Next, you can create a brand style guide that outlines the proper use of your brand assets, including logos, colors, and typography. This will help ensure that your brand identity is consistent across all marketing materials and prevent others from using your brand assets in a way that may damage your brand's reputation.

Finally, it's important to monitor your brand and take legal action against infringers who misuse your brand or intellectual property. For example, if you discover that another company is using your brand name or logo without permission, you can send a cease and desist letter or take legal action to protect your brand's identity.

By taking these legal considerations into account, you can establish a strong and legally protected brand identity for your startup company, helping to ensure its long-term success.

Explanation in the form of a story:
Once upon a time, there was a small business owner named Sarah who had just launched a new line of handmade jewelry. She spent months creating unique designs and perfecting her branding, including a catchy name and a beautiful logo.

Excited about her new business, Sarah began selling her jewelry at local markets and on her website. However, after a few weeks, she received a cease-and-desist letter from a well-established jewelry company claiming that her brand name and logo were too similar to their own.

Feeling confused and frustrated, Sarah realized that she had not done her due diligence in researching existing trademarks before choosing her brand name and logo. She had unintentionally infringed on the other company's intellectual property, putting her business at risk of legal action and damage to her brand reputation.

Sarah quickly hired a trademark attorney and learned about the legal considerations of branding, including the importance of conducting a trademark search and registering her own trademark with the USPTO.

After several months of legal proceedings, Sarah was able to negotiate a settlement with the other company, allowing her to continue using her brand name and logo with some modifications to differentiate it from the other company's brand.

Through this experience, Sarah learned the importance of protecting her brand legally and took proactive steps to ensure that her intellectual property was secured. She registered her trademark, created a comprehensive brand style guide, and regularly monitored her brand to prevent any potential infringement.

As a result of her proactive efforts, Sarah's business continued to grow, and her brand became well-known in the industry, all while avoiding any legal issues.

In summary, legal considerations in branding, including trademarks, copyrights, and intellectual property, are critical to safeguard your brand's identity and prevent infringement by others. By taking proactive steps to protect your brand legally, you can establish a strong brand presence and avoid costly legal disputes.

25

Measuring Your Brand's Success: Metrics and Analytics

Measuring your brand's success is crucial for any business looking to grow and remain competitive in today's marketplace. Metrics and analytics provide insights into the effectiveness of your marketing strategies, customer engagement, and brand perception, enabling you to make data-driven decisions that can drive growth and improve customer satisfaction.

Importance of Measuring Brand Success:

Identifying the Effectiveness of Marketing Strategies:
  Measuring your brand's success allows you to track the performance of your marketing strategies and campaigns. With analytics, you can determine which channels are driving the most traffic, conversions, and engagement. By analyzing the data, you can identify the strengths and weaknesses of each campaign and adjust your strategies accordingly to maximize results.

Understanding Customer Behavior and Engagement:

Measuring metrics and analytics also allows you to gain insights into customer behavior and engagement. By tracking website traffic, social media engagement, and other key metrics, you can identify which content resonates most with your audience and adjust your messaging and tactics to better meet their needs and expectations.

Monitoring Brand Reputation:

Measuring your brand's success also enables you to monitor your brand's reputation online. With analytics, you can track mentions, reviews, and sentiment around your brand on social media, review sites, and other platforms. By addressing negative feedback and responding to customer concerns, you can improve brand perception and build customer loyalty.

How to Measure Brand Success Effectively:

Define Key Metrics:

To measure your brand's success effectively, you need to identify the key metrics that are most important to your business. These could include website traffic, social media engagement, customer retention, or conversion rates. By defining these metrics, you can focus your efforts on tracking and improving the areas that have the greatest impact on your business.

Use Analytics Tools:

There are many analytics tools available that can help you track and measure key metrics. Google Analytics is a popular tool for tracking website traffic and user behavior, while social media management platforms like Hootsuite or Sprout Social can help you monitor social media engagement and brand reputation. By using these tools, you can gain insights into the effectiveness of your marketing strategies and adjust your tactics accordingly.

Monitor Social Media Engagement:

Social media engagement is a crucial metric for measuring your brand's success. By tracking likes, shares, comments, and other forms of engagement, you can determine which content is resonating most with your audience and adjust your messaging and tactics to better meet their needs. You can also monitor brand mentions and sentiment to address negative feedback and improve brand perception.

Track Website Traffic:

Website traffic is another important metric for measuring your brand's success. By tracking the number of visitors, pageviews, and bounce rates, you can determine the effectiveness of your website and identify areas for improvement. You can also track conversion rates to determine which pages and campaigns are driving the most leads and sales.

Quick example:

Define Key Metrics:

The company could define the following key metrics:

Website Traffic: the number of visitors, pageviews, and bounce rates on their website.

Social Media Engagement: the number of likes, comments, shares, and followers on their social media profiles.

Conversion Rates: the percentage of website visitors who make a purchase.

Customer Retention: the percentage of customers who make repeat purchases.

Use Analytics Tools:

The company could use Google Analytics to track website traffic and user behavior. They could also use social media management platforms like Hootsuite to monitor social media engagement and brand reputation.

Monitor Social Media Engagement:

The company could track social media engagement by monitoring likes, comments, shares, and followers on their social media profiles. They could also monitor brand mentions and sentiment to address negative feedback and improve brand perception. For example, if they notice that customers are frequently mentioning their products in a positive way, they can use this feedback to create new content or promotions that speak directly to their audience's interests.

Track Website Traffic:

The company could track website traffic by monitoring the number of visitors, pageviews, and bounce rates on their website. If they notice that certain pages or campaigns are driving more traffic than others, they can adjust their marketing strategies to focus on those areas. For example, if they see that a particular blog post is generating a lot of traffic, they can create more content around that topic to drive more engagement and conversions.

In summary, by defining key metrics, using analytics tools,

monitoring social media engagement, and tracking website traffic, this skincare company can gain valuable insights into the effectiveness of their marketing strategies, customer engagement, and brand perception. By making data-driven decisions based on these insights, they can improve their customer satisfaction and drive growth for their business.

Explanation in the form of a story:

Once upon a time, there was a small business owner named Sarah who ran a boutique clothing store. Sarah was passionate about fashion and had spent years building her brand from scratch. She knew her customers well and took pride in creating a unique shopping experience that kept them coming back for more.

As her business grew, Sarah realized that she needed to measure her brand's success to continue growing and stay competitive. She wanted to understand what was working well and what needed improvement, but she wasn't sure where to start.

Sarah began by defining key metrics that were important to her business, such as website traffic, social media engagement, and customer retention. She started using analytics tools like Google Analytics to track website traffic and user behavior and social media management platforms like Hootsuite to monitor social media engagement and brand reputation.

Through tracking her website traffic, Sarah realized that most of her customers were visiting her site through mobile devices. So, she worked with a web developer to optimize her site for mobile users, which increased website traffic and engagement.

Sarah also monitored social media engagement and found that her customers loved seeing pictures of new arrivals and behind-the-scenes photos of her boutique. She adjusted her social media strategy to focus more on visual content, which resulted in increased engagement and followers.

Lastly, Sarah started tracking customer retention and found that many of her loyal customers were referred by other customers. She started implementing a referral program that rewarded customers for referring their friends, which helped her business grow even more.

Thanks to measuring her brand's success, Sarah was able to identify areas for improvement and adjust her tactics accordingly. Her business continued to thrive, and her loyal customers continued to spread the word about her boutique. She learned that by using metrics and analytics, she could make data-driven decisions that helped her business grow and succeed.

In conclusion, measuring your brand's success is crucial for any business looking to grow and remain competitive in today's marketplace. By defining key metrics, using analytics tools, monitoring social media engagement, and tracking website traffic, you can gain insights into the effectiveness of your marketing strategies, customer engagement, and brand perception, enabling you to make data-driven decisions that can drive growth and improve customer satisfaction.

26

The Future of Branding: Emerging Trends and Technologies

The future of branding is evolving rapidly due to emerging trends and technologies. Today, branding goes beyond logos, slogans, and packaging; it encompasses the entire customer experience, and it's more important than ever. In this response, we'll discuss the emerging trends and technologies that are shaping the future of branding, and we'll offer guidance on how to stay ahead of the curve and incorporate these new developments into your branding strategy.

Personalization:
Personalization is the customization of the customer experience to suit their unique preferences and needs. Personalization is becoming more important in the branding world as customers demand more personalized experiences. Brands can leverage data to personalize their messaging, product recommendations, and customer service to create a more tailored experience. Brands that can offer a personalized experience to customers are more likely to succeed in the

future.

Artificial Intelligence:
Artificial intelligence (AI) is being used in various fields, and branding is no exception. AI can help brands analyze customer data to create more personalized experiences. Chatbots, for example, are being used to improve customer service and enhance the customer experience. AI can also be used to predict consumer behavior and preferences, which can help brands make more informed decisions.

Augmented Reality:
Augmented reality (AR) is a technology that superimposes digital images onto the real world. AR is becoming more prevalent in branding as it can create a more immersive experience for customers. Brands can use AR to showcase their products and services in a more interactive way. For example, a makeup brand could use AR to allow customers to "try on" makeup virtually before making a purchase.

Social Media:
Social media is no longer just a platform for communicating with friends and family; it's also a crucial branding tool. Social media platforms offer brands the opportunity to reach a wider audience and engage with their customers in real-time. Brands can use social media to create communities, share user-generated content, and offer customer support.

Sustainability:
Sustainability is becoming increasingly important to consumers, and brands that prioritize sustainability are more likely

to succeed in the future. Brands can incorporate sustainability into their branding strategy by using eco-friendly materials, reducing their carbon footprint, and supporting social causes.

To stay ahead of the curve and incorporate these new developments into your branding strategy, consider the following:

Stay up to date with emerging trends and technologies:
Brands that stay up to date with emerging trends and technologies are more likely to succeed in the future. Keep an eye on industry news, attend conferences and events, and engage with thought leaders to stay informed.

Invest in technology:

Investing in technology can help brands create more personalized experiences, improve customer service, and enhance the overall customer experience. Consider investing in AI, AR, and other emerging technologies to stay ahead of the curve.

Prioritize sustainability:

Sustainability is becoming increasingly important to consumers, and brands that prioritize sustainability are more likely to succeed in the future. Consider incorporating sustainability into your branding strategy by using eco-friendly materials, reducing your carbon footprint, and supporting social causes.

In conclusion, the future of branding is evolving rapidly, and it's more important than ever. Brands that can offer a personalized experience to customers, incorporate emerging technologies like AI and AR, and prioritize sustainability are more likely to succeed in the future. Stay up to date with emerging trends and technologies, invest in technology, and prioritize sustainability to stay ahead of the curve and incorporate these new developments into your branding strategy.

Quick example:
Personalization:
Nike is a great example of a brand that is using personalization to enhance the customer experience. They launched a personalized shoe platform called Nike By You, which allows customers to design their own shoes based on their preferences. Customers can choose the colors, materials, and even add their own initials or text to the shoe. This platform creates a more personalized experience for customers and has been successful in driving sales for Nike.

Artificial Intelligence:
Domino's Pizza is an example of a brand that is using AI to improve customer service. They launched an AI-powered chatbot called Dom that helps customers place their orders, track their delivery, and answer any questions they may have. This chatbot has improved customer service and has reduced the workload for their customer service team.

Augmented Reality:
Sephora is a beauty retailer that has incorporated AR into their branding strategy. They launched an AR-powered feature called Virtual Artist, which allows customers to try on makeup virtually before making a purchase. This feature has created a more immersive and interactive experience for customers, and has been successful in driving sales for Sephora.

Social Media:

Dove is a brand that has created a strong community on social media. They launched a campaign called #RealBeauty, which celebrates women of all shapes, sizes, and ages. This campaign has created a community of women who support and empower each other, and has been successful in driving brand loyalty for Dove.

Sustainability:

Patagonia is a brand that prioritizes sustainability in their branding strategy. They use eco-friendly materials in their products, and they also donate 1% of their sales to support environmental causes. This commitment to sustainability has resonated with customers and has been successful in driving sales for Patagonia.

These examples illustrate how brands are incorporating the emerging trends and technologies mentioned in the previous answer into their branding strategies. By staying up to date with emerging trends and technologies, investing in technology, and prioritizing sustainability, brands can create a more personalized, immersive, and socially responsible customer experience that drives loyalty and sales.

Explanation in the form of a story:

Once upon a time, there was a small clothing company named "Threads". Threads was a young brand, and it struggled to find its place in the market. The company had a strong mission to create eco-friendly clothing that was also affordable, but it was having difficulty standing out from the competition.

One day, Threads decided to attend a branding conference to learn more about emerging trends and technologies. The conference was full of thought leaders, industry experts, and other brands looking to stay ahead of the curve. Threads listened to keynote speeches, participated in panel discussions, and networked with other attendees.

At the conference, Threads learned about the importance of personalization in the branding world. The company realized that it could use data to personalize its messaging, product recommendations, and customer service to create a more tailored experience for its customers.

Threads also learned about the power of artificial intelligence (AI) in branding. The company realized that AI could help it analyze customer data to create more personalized experiences. Threads decided to invest in AI technology to better understand its customers' preferences and make more informed decisions.

Moreover, Threads discovered the potential of augmented reality (AR) in creating immersive experiences for customers. The company realized that it could use AR to showcase its products and services in a more interactive way. Threads decided to create an AR feature on its website to allow customers to "try on" clothes virtually before making a purchase.

After the conference, Threads realized the importance of social media in the branding world. The company started using social media platforms to engage with its customers, share user-generated content, and offer customer support. Threads created a community around its brand, and it saw an increase in customer loyalty.

Lastly, Threads learned about the importance of sustainability in the branding world. The company realized that consumers were becoming increasingly conscious of the environmental impact of their purchases. Threads decided to incorporate sustainability into its branding strategy by using eco-friendly materials, reducing its carbon footprint, and supporting social causes.

Thanks to attending the branding conference, Threads was able to stay ahead of the curve and incorporate these new developments into its branding strategy. The company created a personalized experience for its customers, invested in AI technology, incorporated AR into its website, engaged with its customers on social media, and prioritized sustainability. As a result, Threads saw an increase in brand recognition and customer loyalty. The small clothing company was no longer struggling to find its place in the market; it was now a leader in the industry.

27

Staying Relevant: How to Evolve Your Brand Over Time

In today's fast-paced and ever-changing market, it is essential to stay relevant to remain competitive. Evolving your brand over time is a critical step in achieving this. By keeping your brand fresh and updated, you can maintain your relevance and adapt to the changing needs of your target audience. In this way, your brand can continue to attract new customers and retain existing ones.

The following are some reasons why it is important to evolve your brand over time:

Market Changes: The market is constantly changing, and so are the needs of consumers. As a result, brands must adapt to these changes to remain relevant and maintain customer loyalty.

Competition: With so many companies competing for the

same audience, it's important to stand out. By evolving your brand, you can differentiate yourself from your competitors and maintain your competitive edge.

Consumer Behavior: As consumer behavior changes, so do their expectations of brands. By keeping up with these changes, you can ensure that your brand remains appealing and relevant to your target audience.

So, how can you refresh and update your brand?

Conduct a Brand Audit: Start by assessing your current brand and identifying areas for improvement. This audit should include your visual identity, messaging, brand values, and target audience.

Redesign Your Visual Identity: Your visual identity, including your logo and color scheme, should evolve with your brand. Consider refreshing your visual identity to reflect your brand's new values, mission, and target audience.

Rebranding: If your brand has become outdated or no longer resonates with your target audience, a complete rebranding may be necessary. This involves a complete overhaul of your brand's visual identity, messaging, and values.

Update Your Messaging: Your messaging should reflect your brand's values and resonate with your target audience. Consider updating your messaging to reflect your brand's new direction and values.

Embrace New Technology: Technology is constantly evolving, and brands that keep up with the latest trends can remain relevant. Consider incorporating new technology into your brand, such as social media, mobile apps, or augmented reality.

Quick example:
Apple is one of the world's leading technology companies, known for its innovative products and exceptional branding. However, the brand that we know today is the result of significant evolution over the years. Here are some of the key ways Apple has evolved its brand:

Redesigned its logo: Apple's logo has undergone several redesigns since its inception in 1977. The company started with a rainbow-colored apple with a bite taken out of it, which evolved into a more streamlined, monochrome version in the late 1990s. In 2013, the company updated the logo again, making it even simpler and flatter.

Rebranded itself as a lifestyle brand: Apple started as a computer company, but as it expanded into other areas such as music and mobile devices, it rebranded itself as a lifestyle brand. The company now focuses on creating products that are not just functional but also stylish and aspirational.

Evolved its messaging: Apple's messaging has evolved over the years, from the famous "Think Different" campaign in the 1990s to more recent messaging that focuses on the company's commitment to privacy and sustainability.

Embraced new technology: Apple has always been at the

forefront of new technology, and it continues to embrace new trends such as augmented reality and artificial intelligence. The company also regularly updates its products to stay current with the latest technology.

Overall, Apple's evolution is a great example of how a brand can stay relevant over time by refreshing its visual identity, messaging, and values. By embracing new technology and rebranding itself as a lifestyle brand, Apple has remained one of the most innovative and successful companies in the world.

Explanation in the form of a story:
Once upon a time, there was a clothing company that had been in business for over a decade. They had a loyal customer base, but sales had been declining over the years. They knew that they needed to do something to stay relevant and attract new customers, but they weren't sure where to start.

The company decided to conduct a brand audit to assess their current position and identify areas for improvement. They discovered that their visual identity was outdated and no longer resonated with their target audience. The logo and color scheme were old-fashioned, and their messaging didn't reflect the company's values or mission.

The company decided to refresh their visual identity by re-designing their logo and color scheme. They worked with a branding agency to create a new logo that was modern, bold, and memorable. They also updated their color scheme to be more vibrant and eye-catching.

In addition to refreshing their visual identity, the company decided to update their messaging to better reflect their values and mission. They worked on creating a new tagline that emphasized their commitment to sustainability and ethical sourcing. They also developed a new brand voice that was more conversational and relatable.

The company embraced new technology as well. They developed a mobile app that allowed customers to browse their products and make purchases directly from their phones. They also started using social media to connect with their audience and showcase their new brand identity.

As a result of these changes, the company was able to attract a new audience while retaining their existing customers. Sales increased, and the company's brand reputation improved. They became known as a company that was committed to sustainability and ethical practices, which resonated with their audience.

In conclusion, the clothing company was able to evolve their brand over time and stay relevant in a changing market. By conducting a brand audit, refreshing their visual identity, updating their messaging, and embracing new technology, they were able to attract new customers and retain their existing ones. This helped them remain competitive and successful in the long run.

In conclusion, evolving your brand over time is critical to staying relevant in today's ever-changing market. By refreshing your brand's visual identity, messaging, and values, you can maintain your competitive edge and attract new customers while retaining existing ones.

28

Lessons from Successful Phoenix Brands: Case Studies and Examples

Phoenix brands are those that have risen from the ashes of failure and reinvented themselves to become successful again. These brands have been able to reimagine themselves, redefine their brand identity, and re-engage with their target audience. In this article, we'll explore some examples of successful Phoenix brands and the lessons that can be learned from their experiences.

Apple: One of the most famous Phoenix brands is Apple. In the mid-1990s, Apple was struggling to stay afloat. But, after the return of Steve Jobs, the brand underwent a complete overhaul. Apple redefined its brand identity by focusing on design, innovation, and simplicity. Today, Apple is one of the most valuable companies in the world, with a loyal customer base that trusts the brand to deliver quality products.

Lesson: Reimagining your brand identity can help you redefine your brand's values and differentiate yourself from competitors.

Lego: In the early 2000s, Lego was facing a crisis. The company was losing money, and its traditional toys were becoming less popular with children. Lego responded by launching a new product line aimed at young adults. The Lego Mindstorms line allowed customers to build and program their own robots, giving the brand a new image as a cutting-edge technology company.

Lesson: It's important to listen to your customers and adapt to their changing needs and interests.

Nintendo: In the mid-2000s, Nintendo was losing market share to competitors like Microsoft and Sony. In response, the company launched the Wii, a gaming console that used motion-sensing technology to create a new type of gaming experience. The Wii became a huge success, and Nintendo's brand image was transformed from a niche player to a main-stream entertainment company.

Lesson: Innovation is key to staying ahead of the competition and engaging with new customers.

Old Spice: Old Spice is a classic brand that has been around for over 80 years. However, in the early 2000s, the brand was struggling to connect with a younger audience. Old Spice decided to reinvent itself by launching a new marketing campaign aimed at young men. The "Smell Like a Man, Man" campaign featured humorous ads that went viral, and Old Spice's sales increased dramatically.

Lesson: Humor and creativity can be powerful tools for engaging with customers and creating a memorable brand image.

Netflix: Netflix started as a DVD rental service in the late 1990s, but quickly adapted to changing technology and consumer preferences. The company transitioned to a streaming service in the mid-2000s and began producing its own content in the 2010s. Today, Netflix is one of the most popular entertainment platforms in the world, with a brand image that is synonymous with quality content.

Lesson: Adapt to new technology and consumer preferences, and don't be afraid to take risks and innovate.

Quick example:

Old Spice is a classic brand that has been around for over 80 years, but by the early 2000s, the brand was struggling to connect with a younger audience. To revitalize its brand, Old Spice decided to take a humorous approach to its marketing and launched a new campaign aimed at young men. The "Smell Like a Man, Man" campaign featured a series of humorous ads that went viral, featuring actor Isaiah Mustafa as the "Old Spice Guy."

The ads were a huge success, generating millions of views on YouTube and other social media platforms. The campaign's success allowed Old Spice to redefine its brand identity, positioning itself as a humorous, irreverent brand that could appeal to younger consumers.

Old Spice's reinvention was a major success, with the brand's sales increasing dramatically after the launch of the "Smell Like a Man, Man" campaign. The brand continued to build on this success with subsequent campaigns, including the "Believe in Your Smell" campaign, which featured an interactive website and social media campaign that allowed customers to create their own personalized Old Spice ads.

The lesson here is that humor and creativity can be powerful tools for engaging with customers and creating a memorable brand image. By taking a bold approach to its marketing, Old Spice was able to differentiate itself from competitors and reconnect with a younger audience. This example shows that even established brands can reinvent themselves and stay relevant by redefining their brand identity and adapting to changing customer preferences.

Explanation in the form of a story:

Once upon a time, there was a struggling company called XYZ. XYZ had been in business for many years, but they were losing market share to competitors and struggling to stay afloat. Customers were no longer interested in XYZ's products, and the company's brand image had become stale and outdated.

One day, the CEO of XYZ decided to take a bold step. He hired a team of marketing experts and tasked them with reimagining the company's brand identity. The marketing team spent weeks researching the market and listening to customer feedback. They realized that customers wanted products that were innovative, easy to use, and focused on sustainability.

The marketing team came up with a new brand identity for XYZ that centered around these values. They created a new product line that used cutting-edge technology to reduce waste and improve usability. They launched a new marketing campaign that highlighted the company's commitment to sustainability and innovation.

At first, the changes were met with skepticism from customers and the industry. But slowly, word began to spread about XYZ's new direction. Customers started to take notice of the company's innovative products and commitment to sustainability. The company's sales began to rise, and soon, XYZ was back on the path to success.

The CEO of XYZ realized that the key to success was not to cling to the old ways of doing things, but to adapt to changing customer needs and embrace innovation. He learned that by reimagining his company's brand identity and redefining its values, he could connect with customers in a meaningful way and differentiate his brand from competitors.

In the end, XYZ became a successful phoenix brand, rising from the ashes of failure to become a leader in its industry. And the CEO learned that sometimes, the best way to move forward is to take a step back and look at your brand with fresh eyes, willing to make the necessary changes to stay relevant and successful.

In conclusion, these examples of successful Phoenix brands demonstrate that it's possible to reinvent your brand and come back stronger after a period of failure. By reimagining your brand identity, adapting to changing customer needs, innovating, using humor and creativity, and staying ahead of the competition, you can build a strong brand that connects with customers and stands the test of time.

29

Overcoming Branding Challenges: Common Pitfalls and How to Avoid Them

Branding is a crucial aspect of any business as it establishes the company's identity and sets it apart from competitors. However, branding challenges are common and can negatively impact a company's reputation and sales. In this response, I will discuss some common branding challenges and pitfalls and provide guidance on how to avoid them.

Lack of differentiation:
One of the most common branding challenges is creating a brand that is not unique or different from competitors. In today's competitive business environment, it's crucial to differentiate your brand from others to stand out in the market. To avoid this pitfall, research your competitors and identify their strengths and weaknesses. Use this information to develop a unique value proposition that differentiates your brand. You can also differentiate your brand by creating a

unique visual identity that stands out from others in the market.

Negative feedback:

Another significant branding challenge is dealing with negative feedback. Negative feedback can damage a brand's reputation and impact sales. To avoid this pitfall, it's crucial to listen to your customers and address their concerns. Respond to negative feedback promptly and professionally, and take steps to address any issues raised. By doing so, you demonstrate that you care about your customers and are committed to delivering high-quality products or services.

Inconsistent branding:

Consistency is key to establishing a strong brand identity. Inconsistent branding can confuse customers and make it challenging to establish brand recognition. To avoid this pitfall, develop a comprehensive brand style guide that outlines your brand's visual identity, tone of voice, and messaging. Ensure that all marketing materials, including social media posts, emails, and advertisements, adhere to this style guide. Doing so will help establish a consistent brand identity and make it easier for customers to recognize your brand.

Lack of brand awareness:

Another significant branding challenge is a lack of brand awareness. If customers are not aware of your brand, it can be challenging to establish a loyal customer base and increase sales. To avoid this pitfall, invest in marketing efforts that increase brand awareness, such as social media advertising, content marketing, and influencer partnerships. These efforts can help increase brand recognition and establish your brand as a leader in the market.

In conclusion, overcoming branding challenges requires careful planning, research, and a commitment to delivering high-quality products and services. By avoiding common pitfalls such as lack of differentiation, negative feedback, inconsistent branding, and lack of brand awareness, businesses can establish a strong brand identity and stand out in today's competitive market.

Quick example:
Lack of differentiation:

Suppose you are starting a new coffee shop in a crowded market where there are already several established coffee shops. To differentiate your brand, you could focus on offering unique blends of coffee or specialize in a particular type of coffee, such as artisanal or organic coffee. You could also create a unique visual identity, such as a logo or store design, that stands out from other coffee shops.

Negative feedback:

Imagine you are a small e-commerce business selling hand-made jewelry online. If a customer leaves a negative review, it's important to respond to their feedback in a prompt and professional manner. You could acknowledge their concerns, apologize for any issues they experienced, and offer a solution, such as a refund or replacement. By addressing negative feedback in this way, you demonstrate to customers that you are committed to providing excellent customer service.

Inconsistent branding:

Suppose you are a marketing manager for a fashion brand, and you want to ensure that all marketing materials adhere to a consistent brand identity. You could develop a comprehensive style guide that outlines the brand's visual identity, including colors, typography, and photography style. You could also create guidelines for tone of voice and messaging to ensure that all marketing materials have a consistent brand voice.

Lack of brand awareness:

Imagine you are a startup tech company looking to increase brand awareness. You could invest in content marketing efforts, such as blogging or creating videos, to showcase your expertise and build your reputation as a thought leader in your industry. You could also collaborate with influencers or industry experts to promote your brand and reach a wider audience. Additionally, you could invest in social media advertising to increase brand visibility and drive traffic to your website.

Explanation in the form of a story:

Once upon a time, there was a small business that sold handmade soaps. The owner, Sarah, was passionate about creating all-natural and organic soaps that were gentle on the skin. She spent months perfecting her recipe and designing unique packaging that reflected her brand's values.

However, Sarah soon realized that she was facing some significant branding challenges. She discovered that her soaps were similar to those sold by larger competitors, and her brand was not standing out in the market. Despite her best efforts, she was struggling to gain traction and attract new customers.

Sarah knew she needed to differentiate her brand to stand out in the market. She researched her competitors and found that they were not as focused on using organic and all-natural ingredients. She decided to highlight this as a unique value proposition for her brand and emphasized the benefits of using her soaps.

However, Sarah soon encountered another branding challenge. She received negative feedback from customers who were unhappy with the scent of her soaps. Instead of ignoring the feedback or becoming defensive, Sarah took the feedback seriously and worked on improving the scent of her soaps. She also made sure to respond to every customer's feedback in a professional and courteous manner.

Over time, Sarah's efforts paid off, and her brand began to gain traction. However, she realized that her branding efforts were not consistent. Her social media posts did not match the tone and messaging of her website, and her packaging had a different design than her website.

To address this inconsistency, Sarah created a comprehensive brand style guide that outlined her brand's visual identity, tone of voice, and messaging. She ensured that all her marketing materials, including social media posts, emails, and advertisements, adhered to this style guide. This helped establish a consistent brand identity and made it easier for customers to recognize her brand.

As Sarah's brand awareness increased, she continued to invest in marketing efforts that increased brand awareness. She partnered with influencers in the organic beauty space and started offering free samples to customers. Her efforts paid off, and her small business grew to become a successful brand that was recognized for its high-quality, all-natural soaps.

In conclusion, Sarah's journey highlights the importance of overcoming branding challenges to establish a successful business. By addressing common branding pitfalls such as lack of differentiation, negative feedback, inconsistent branding, and lack of brand awareness, businesses can create a strong brand identity that stands out in the market.

30

Conclusion: Bringing Your Phoenix Brand to Life.

"Phoenix Branding: A No-Nonsense Guide to Building Your Own Brand Identity" is an insightful book that guides readers on how to create and establish their brand. The book highlights the importance of branding and how it can positively impact the success of a business.

The key themes and takeaways from the book are:

1. Understanding the concept of branding: Branding is the process of creating a unique identity for your business that differentiates it from its competitors. A strong brand is essential for building a loyal customer base and establishing a positive reputation in the market.
2. Developing your brand strategy: A well-defined brand strategy is crucial to the success of your business. This involves identifying your target audience, understanding their needs and preferences, and creating a brand message that resonates with them.
3. Crafting your brand identity: A brand identity is a

combination of visual and verbal elements that represent your brand. It includes your logo, color palette, font, and brand voice. It is important to create a consistent and memorable brand identity that aligns with your brand message.

4. Building brand awareness: Building brand awareness is essential to attract new customers and establish your brand in the market. This can be achieved through various marketing and advertising strategies such as social media, email marketing, influencer marketing, and paid advertising.

5. Maintaining brand consistency: Consistency is key to building a strong brand. This involves ensuring that all aspects of your brand, including messaging, visual identity, and customer experience, are consistent across all platforms.

To bring your own phoenix brand to life, here are some final guidance and inspiration:

1. Know your audience: Understanding your target audience is crucial to creating a brand that resonates with them. Conduct market research and customer surveys to gain insights into their needs, preferences, and behaviors.

2. Define your brand message: Your brand message should communicate the unique value proposition of your business. Identify your brand's mission, vision, and core values, and use them to create a compelling brand message.

3. Create a memorable visual identity: Your brand's visual identity should be consistent, memorable, and representative of your brand message. Hire a professional designer

to create a logo, color palette, and font that aligns with your brand's personality and values.

4. Build brand awareness: Use various marketing and advertising strategies to build brand awareness and attract new customers. Leverage social media, influencer marketing, and paid advertising to reach your target audience.

5. Maintain consistency: Consistency is key to building a strong brand. Ensure that all aspects of your brand, including messaging, visual identity, and customer experience, are consistent across all platforms.

6. Evolve and adapt: As your business grows and evolves, your brand should also adapt to changing market conditions and customer needs. Continuously monitor your brand performance and make adjustments as necessary.

In conclusion, creating a phoenix brand takes time, effort, and commitment. By understanding the key themes and takeaways from this book and following the guidance and inspiration provided, you can bring your own phoenix brand to life and establish a strong brand identity that resonates with your target audience.

Quick example:

Let's say that you want to start a business selling handmade candles. Here are the steps you might take to create your phoenix brand:

Know your audience: Conduct market research to identify your target audience. In this case, your audience might be people who enjoy using eco-friendly and natural products, who have an interest in home decor, and who are willing to pay a premium for high-quality, handmade candles.

Define your brand message: Based on your audience research, you might develop a brand message that emphasizes your commitment to using all-natural, eco-friendly ingredients and your passion for creating unique, high-quality candles that enhance the ambiance of any room.

Create a memorable visual identity: Hire a professional designer to create a logo, color palette, and font that reflect your brand message. Your logo might feature an image of a candle or flame, and your color palette might include earthy tones to emphasize the natural aspect of your product.

Build brand awareness: Use social media platforms like Instagram and Facebook to showcase your products and build a following. You might also consider partnering with influencers or bloggers who cater to your target audience to help spread the word about your brand.

Maintain consistency: Ensure that all aspects of your brand, including messaging, visual identity, and customer experience, are consistent across all platforms. This includes packaging, website design, and customer service.

Evolve and adapt: As your business grows and evolves, stay attuned to the needs and preferences of your audience. You might consider expanding your product line to include other home decor items, or offering custom candle-making services.

By following these steps, you can create a strong phoenix

brand that resonates with your target audience and helps your business stand out in a crowded market.

Explanation in the form of a story:

Once upon a time, there was a young entrepreneur named Sarah who had a vision to start her own business. She had a passion for baking and wanted to share her delicious treats with the world. However, she quickly realized that there were many other bakeries in her area and it would be difficult to stand out from the competition.

Sarah knew that branding was important, but she didn't know where to start. She began to research and read books about branding and marketing, including "Phoenix Branding: A No-Nonsense Guide to Building Your Own Brand Identity." As she read the book, she discovered the key themes and takeaways that would help her create her own phoenix brand.

First, Sarah learned the importance of understanding the concept of branding. She realized that creating a unique identity for her business was essential to differentiating herself from the competition. She also learned the importance of developing a brand strategy and creating a brand message that resonated with her target audience.

Next, Sarah began to craft her brand identity. She worked with a professional designer to create a memorable logo, color palette, and font that aligned with her brand's personality and values. She also developed a brand voice that was consistent with her brand message.

With her brand identity in place, Sarah began to build brand awareness. She created a website and social media accounts to showcase her products and engage with her customers. She also used email marketing and paid advertising to reach her target audience.

Throughout the process, Sarah made sure to maintain consistency in all aspects of her brand. She ensured that her messaging, visual identity, and customer experience were consistent across all platforms. She also adapted her brand as her business grew and evolved.

As a result of her efforts, Sarah's bakery became a huge success. Her customers loved her delicious treats and her brand became well-known in her community. Sarah's phoenix brand had come to life, and she was proud of the unique identity she had created for her business.

www.ingramcontent.com/pod-product-compliance
Lightning Source LLC
Chambersburg PA
CBHW070636220526
45466CB00001B/198